"NOBODY'S CHILDREN":

Jamaican Children in Police Detention and Government Institutions

Human Rights Watch
New York • Washington • London • Brussels

ISBN: 1-56432-230-0
Library of Congress Catalog Card Number: 99-63489

Cover design by Rafael Jiménez

Addresses for Human Rights Watch
350 Fifth Avenue, 34th Floor, New York, NY 10118-3299
Tel: (212) 290-4700, Fax: (212) 736-1300, E-mail: hrwnyc@hrw.org

1522 K Street, N.W., #910, Washington, DC 20005-1202
Tel: (202) 371-6592, Fax: (202) 371-0124, E-mail: hrwdc@hrw.org

33 Islington High Street, N1 9LH London, UK
Tel: (171) 713-1995, Fax: (171) 713-1800, E-mail: hrwatchuk@gn.apc.org

15 Rue Van Campenhout, 1000 Brussels, Belgium
Tel: (2) 732-2009, Fax: (2) 732-0471, E-mail:hrwatcheu@skynet.be

Web Site Address: http://www.hrw.org

Listserv address: To subscribe to the list, send an e-mail message to
majordomo@igc.apc.org with "subscribe hrw-news" in the body of the message
(leave the subject line blank).

Human Rights Watch is dedicated to
protecting the human rights of people around the world.

We stand with victims and activists to prevent
discrimination, to uphold political freedom, to protect people from inhumane
conduct in wartime, and to bring offenders to justice.

We investigate and expose
human rights violations and hold abusers accountable.

We challenge governments and those who hold power to end abusive practices
and respect international human rights law.

We enlist the public and the international
community to support the cause of human rights for all.

HUMAN RIGHTS WATCH

Human Rights Watch conducts regular, systematic investigations of human rights abuses in some seventy countries around the world. Our reputation for timely, reliable disclosures has made us an essential source of information for those concerned with human rights. We address the human rights practices of governments of all political stripes, of all geopolitical alignments, and of all ethnic and religious persuasions. Human Rights Watch defends freedom of thought and expression, due process and equal protection of the law, and a vigorous civil society; we document and denounce murders, disappearances, torture, arbitrary imprisonment, discrimination, and other abuses of internationally recognized human rights. Our goal is to hold governments accountable if they transgress the rights of their people.

Human Rights Watch began in 1978 with the founding of its Europe and Central Asia division (then known as Helsinki Watch). Today, it also includes divisions covering Africa, the Americas, Asia, and the Middle East. In addition, it includes three thematic divisions on arms, children's rights, and women's rights. It maintains offices in New York, Washington, Los Angeles, London, Brussels, Moscow, Dushanbe, Rio de Janeiro, and Hong Kong. Human Rights Watch is an independent, nongovernmental organization, supported by contributions from private individuals and foundations worldwide. It accepts no government funds, directly or indirectly.

The staff includes Kenneth Roth, executive director; Michele Alexander, development director; Reed Brody, advocacy director; Carroll Bogert, communications director; Cynthia Brown, program director; Barbara Guglielmo, finance and administration director; Jeri Laber, special advisor; Lotte Leicht, Brussels office director; Patrick Minges, publications director; Susan Osnos, associate director; Jemera Rone, counsel; Wilder Tayler, general counsel; and Joanna Weschler, United Nations representative. Jonathan Fanton is the chair of the board. Robert L. Bernstein is the founding chair.

The regional directors of Human Rights Watch are Peter Takirambudde, Africa; José Miguel Vivanco, Americas; Sidney Jones, Asia; Holly Cartner, Europe and Central Asia; and Hanny Megally, Middle East and North Africa. The thematic division directors are Joost R. Hiltermann, arms; Lois Whitman, children's; and Regan Ralph, women's.

The members of the board of directors are Jonathan Fanton, chair; Lisa Anderson, Robert L. Bernstein, William Carmichael, Dorothy Cullman, Gina Despres, Irene Diamond, Adrian W. DeWind, Fiona Druckenmiller, Edith Everett, Michael E. Gellert, Vartan Gregorian, Alice H. Henkin, James F. Hoge, Stephen L. Kass, Marina Pinto Kaufman, Bruce Klatsky, Josh Mailman, Yolanda T. Moses, Samuel K. Murumba, Andrew Nathan, Jane Olson, Peter Osnos, Kathleen Peratis, Bruce Rabb, Sigrid Rausing, Orville Schell, Sid Sheinberg, Gary G. Sick, Malcolm Smith, Domna Stanton, and Maya Wiley. Robert L. Bernstein is the founding chair of Human Rights Watch.

ACKNOWLEDGMENTS

This report is based on research conducted in Jamaica from late August to early September 1998 by Rosa Ehrenreich, Clovene Hanchard, Glenn McGrory, and Robert Sloane. (Rosa Ehrenreich is the Acting Director of the Orville H. Schell, Jr. Center for International Human Rights at Yale Law School and the faculty instructor of the Lowenstein International Human Rights Clinic. Glenn McGrory and Robert Sloane are members of the Yale Law School Class of 2000, and Clovene Hanchard is a member of the Yale Medical School Class of 1999). The report was written by Rosa Ehrenreich, Clovene Hanchard, Glenn McGrory, and Robert Sloane, and edited by Lois Whitman, the director of the Children's Rights Division, and Michael McClintock, Deputy Program Director. Sarah DeCosse of the Human Rights Watch Americas Division and Joanne Mariner of the General Counsel's Office provided additional helpful comments on the manuscript.

We wish to thank the Government of Jamaica for providing us with helpful background information and access to government facilities where children are detained. In particular, we are grateful to Winston Bowen, the Director of Children's Services, to Claudette Hemmings, the Deputy Director of Children's Services, and to Ambassador Marjorie Taylor, Minister of State and Special Envoy on Children, all of whom were extremely generous with their time and assistance. We also wish to thank Colonel John Prescott, Director of the Jamaican Department of Correctional Services, June Jarrett, Director of Juvenile Institutions, and Francis Forbes, Commissioner of the Jamaica Constabulary Force. We are also grateful to the numerous members of the Jamaica Constabulary Force who provided access to police lockups and who patiently answered our questions.

In Kingston, many people provided us with helpful background information. In particular, we wish to thank Lloyd Barnett, Dennis Daly, Nancy Anderson, Hilaire Sobers, Leo Aquiano, Carol Samuels, Afshan Khan, Judge Soares of the Kingston Family Court, Father Richard Albert, Reverend Norbert Stephens, Claudette Parris, Sipzroy Bryan, and Neville Webb.

Finally, we wish to thank the many Jamaican children who told us their stories. In this report, we have changed their names to protect their privacy.

TABLE OF CONTENTS

I. SUMMARY 8

II. RECOMMENDATIONS 16
    To the Government of Jamaica 16
        Legal Reform 16
        Police Detention of Children 16
        Children in Detention and Custody, Generally 17
        Access of Children to Counsel and to the Courts 18
        Other Recommendations to the Jamaican Government 19
    To the Jamaican Constabulary 19
    To the Department of Children's Services 20
    To the Department of Correctional Services 21
    To the United Nations 21
    To Donor Governments 22

III. BACKGROUND 23
    A Context of Rising Juvenile Crime 24
        Political Violence and the Emergence of Youth Gangs . . . 25
        Relations Between the Urban Poor and
        Jamaica's Constabulary 27
        Agencies With Responsibility for Children 28
            The Role of the Police 28
            The Children's Services Division 29
            The Department of Correctional Services 30
        Relevant Legal Standards 30
        International Legal Standards 30
            Protection from Violence, Injury, and Neglect . . . 31
            Access to Health Care, Education,
            and Recreation 32
            Rights of Children Accused of
            Criminal Offenses 32
            Rights of Children in Detention 33
        Domestic Legal Standards 35
            The Jamaican Constitution (1962) 35
            The Juveniles Act of 1951 35
            Legal Aid 38
        Jamaica's 1993 Report to the U.N. Committee on the
        Rights of the Child 39

IV. POLICE LOCKUPS 41
   "Adult" Lockups 41
      Spanish Town 41
      Kingston Central 43
      Halfway Tree 46
      Gun Court 47
   "Juvenile Lockups" 48
      Ewarton Police Station and Juvenile Lockup 49
      Matilda's Corner Police Station and Juvenile Lockup 51
   Evidence About Other Police Lockups 52

Intentional Police Abuse 58
      Physical and Sexual Abuse 59
      Neglect, Rough Treatment, Mental Abuse 61
      Inadequate Responses to Police Abuse 62

V. CHILDREN IN OTHER
   STATE-APPROVED INSTITUTIONS 63
   Children's Services Institutions 63
      Musgrave Children's Home 65
      Glenhope Place of Safety 66
      Glenhope Nursery 67
      Homestead Place of Safety 67
   Correctional Institutions 69
      St. Andrew Remand Center 71

VI. THE SYSTEM AND HOW IT BREAKS DOWN 73
   Structural Shortcomings 73
   System Failures 75

VII. CONCLUSION 79

VIII. APPENDICES 80
   APPENDIX A. U.N. Convention on the Rights of the Child 80
   APPENDIX B. U.N. Rules for the Protection of Juveniles
      Deprived of Their Liberty 103
   APPENDIX C. U.N. Standard Minimum Rules for the Administration
      of Juvenile Justice 120
   APPENDIX D. United Nations Guidelines for the Prevention of
      Juvenile Delinquency 146
   APPENDIX E. Excerpts from The Jamaican Juveniles Act 157

I. SUMMARY

"[T]hem beat the little man, the juvenile, them beat him and kick his head, them kick him into gate and step on him throat . . . . [T]hem carry him gone from [here] last night . . . Inspector Robbie, him there, but him say nothing...."

> — Clive, describing the beating of a young fellow detainee by police

"The cell was tiny, and it was full of feces, bugs, and garbage. I slept on a piece of cardboard on the floor. It was like sleeping in a toilet."

> — Wilbur, age sixteen

In the island nation of Jamaica, many children—often as young as twelve or thirteen—are detained for long periods, sometimes six months or more, in filthy and overcrowded police lockups, in spite of international standards and Jamaican laws that forbid such treatment. The children are often held in the same cells as adults accused of serious crimes, vulnerable to victimization by their cellmates and to ill-treatment by abusive police; and virtually always, they are held in poor conditions, deprived of proper sanitary facilities, adequate ventilation, adequate food, exercise, education, and basic medical care. Some of these children have not been detained on suspicion of criminal activity but have been locked up only because they are deemed "in need of care and protection."

Human Rights Watch visited five working police lockups in Jamaica in late August to early September 1998 and interviewed more than thirty children about their experiences in the lockups. About half of the children we spoke to were in lockups at the time of the interviews, and the remaining children were interviewed after their transfer from police lockups to other government institutions.

All of the lockups we visited were appallingly filthy, with damp, urine-covered floors, virtually no ventilation, and poor or nonexistent lighting. Prisoners were crammed together into tiny cells: in the case of one lockup, for instance, 138 prisoners (including numerous seventeen-year-olds, at least three sixteen-year-olds, and a fifteen-year-old) were crowded into ten cells with a stated maximum capacity of fifty prisoners. Each ten-by-ten-foot cell contained between eleven and fourteen prisoners, although each cell had only one concrete bunk.

Prisoners had no bedding materials but slept instead on tattered and filthy bits of newspaper and cardboard or on the damp concrete floor itself. Because of the lack of ventilation, prisoners had no respite from the extreme heat. The stench in the cells was overpowering—with access to functional toilets severely restricted by the guards, prisoners had little choice but to urinate and defecate in the cells.

Human Rights Watch found that children detained in police lockups remain in their overcrowded cells twenty-four hours a day, let out, if at all, only for court dates and for once-daily trips to the filthy toilet and showers. There are no exercise facilities. The children receive no education at all and have reading materials only if books are brought in by family members. In many lockups, the dim lighting (at times near-darkness, even during the day) makes reading impossible anyway.

No lockups have doctors on the premises or regular visits from medical practitioners; detained children are given health care only in emergencies—and even then only if the police are willing to transport a sick or wounded child to the hospital, which they do not always do. Several of the children we met were visibly injured or ill, but most had received no medical attention. Most prisoners told Human Rights Watch that they must rely on visits from family members to get enough food, as the food supplied in the lockups is limited and of poor quality. In some lockups, children reported going for several days with no food at all, or with only bread or buns.

Children held in lockups are at risk of being victimized by adults. Those children detained in cells with adults are often the prey of older prisoners; although some of the children interviewed reported no major problems in this area, others told us that they had been beaten, raped, and stabbed by older prisoners. Many children (and adult prisoners) told Human Rights Watch of deliberate physical and mental abuse by the police. In the case of children, mental and emotional abuse ranged from "rough talk" (insults and threats) to mock executions. Physical abuse ranged from being pushed around to severe beatings. One fifteen-year-old girl told us that she had been raped by a police officer while held in a lockup overnight.

At any given time, over 90 percent of the prisoners in police lockups are "remand prisoners," pretrial detainees held in detention because bail has not been granted or because they cannot afford the bail set. This is as true for children as for other prisoners.[1] Many of the children we met had no lawyers, and those with

---

[1] In fact, while it remains possible that some children detained improperly in police lockups have been sentenced and not yet transferred, as required, to a juvenile correctional center, all of the children interviewed in the lockups visited by Human Rights Watch were pretrial detainees.

lawyers (generally court-appointed) told us that they spoke with their attorneys rarely, if at all, and often only moments before appearing in court.

After conviction, prisoners are sent to a penitentiary, or, in the case of children, to a juvenile correctional center. Reports indicate that although conditions in Jamaican prisons are also poor, prisons generally have at least minimal exercise and vocational activities and are not as severely overcrowded as the police lockups. Ironically, then, children who are pretrial detainees— presumed innocent—are held in far worse conditions than convicted criminals.

Not all children in police lockups are accused of criminal offenses, however. Some are detained simply for status offenses—acts that would not be crimes if committed by adults, such as truancy, running away from home, or being "uncontrollable". Others are detained because they have been abused or neglected and await permanent placement in appropriate institutions.

In Jamaica, children detained by the authorities generally fall into one of two categories: (1) children suspected of committing a criminal offense; (2) children thought to be "in need of care and protection" (i.e., children who authorities feel are neglected, abused, or "uncontrollable" by parents or guardians).

Under Jamaican law detained children (regardless of whether they have been accused of a crime or are in need of care and protection) are in most cases supposed to be sent to a "place of safety" (a nonsecure short-term institutional care facility run either by the Children's Services Division or by a charitable organization under government supervision) while waiting for a court to arrive at some decision about their case. Only children suspected or convicted of extremely serious and violent offenses—or children whose behavior makes them appear to be a serious threat to others—are supposed to be placed in maximum security settings.

Nonetheless, many children who are abused, neglected, or accused of only petty offenses remain in police lockups for long periods: we met one thirteen-year-old boy, for instance, who had been held in a police lockup for eight months after being accused of stealing a radio. Police officials told Human Rights Watch that the boy had been held for so long not because of his alleged theft, but because he had no family able to care for him and was therefore "in need of care and protection." Despite this, the boy was treated like a criminal and housed in a crowded and filthy police cell rather than in a facility specially designed for the care of children.

Human Rights Watch found that conditions in the facilities run by the Jamaica Children's Services Division (which include "places of safety" and "children's homes") and by the Correctional Services Department (which include the Juvenile Remand Center) were much better than in the police lockups.

While the Remand Center is high security, the places of safety and children's homes are nonsecure facilities. In all these facilities, children slept in dormitories rather than in cells, with each dormitory room housing, in general, ten to fifteen children. Rooms in these facilities were often somewhat shabby, and some displayed a great deal of broken-down furniture and fixtures (in one place of safety, for instance, about two thirds of the sinks and toilets appeared to be broken). Nonetheless, facilities appeared reasonably clean, and trained staff included social workers and teachers; facilities offered vocational and academic classes, counseling, and exercise opportunities.

These facilities could all bear substantial improvement, as Jamaican government officials readily acknowledged. In particular, intake procedures and the provision of physical and mental health care could be greatly improved. Similarly, some children complained of abusive treatment from staff and other children.

On the whole, however, we did not encounter many reports of serious abuses occurring at the Remand Center, children's homes, or places of safety, and conditions seemed to be adequate. To the degree that abuses occur in these facilities, they appear to be occasional rather than systematic. The most serious abuses occur while children are in police custody.

In 1994, Human Rights Watch published a report on children in Jamaican police lockups that documented atrocious conditions similar to those that are to be found today.[2] Although several interviewees in the Jamaican nongovernmental organization (NGO) community told us that conditions in lockups improved slightly in the wake of the 1994 report, and our own findings suggest that the Jamaican police have made some attempt to keep children from being held in cells with adults, the improvements have been minor and largely skin deep. Four years after we first investigated the situation of children in police lockups, the Jamaican government has made little real progress.

Wilbur's Story

"Wilbur"[3] was sixteen when he was interviewed by Human Rights Watch researchers at the St. Andrew's Juvenile Remand Center. An extraordinarily articulate boy, Wilbur, who spent roughly a month in various police lockups before being sent to the Remand Center, told us his story in great detail. It illustrates many

---

[2]Human Rights Watch/Americas and Human Rights Watch Children's Rights Project, *Jamaica: Children Improperly Detained in Police Lockups* (New York, Human Rights Watch, 1994).

[3]Not his real name. Throughout this report, the names of children we met have been changed to protect the children's privacy.

of the hardships faced by impoverished Jamaican children unlucky enough to come into contact with the police or the courts:

> Now I'm here because the court says that I'm in need of care and protection. But the reason the police found me first was that I was arrested for larceny and breaking and entering. After that I was in many lockups. First, Annatto Bay, then Castleton, then Oracabessa. In Annatto Bay, I was in a cell with three guys, all adults. It was very dark, with very limited air, just coming in from small holes. It smelled like fear.
>
> I wasn't there long before I was transferred to the lockup at Oracabessa, which was horrible. The first night—maybe it was just unfortunate. When I went in, they had two cells. The first was filled up with drugs the police had seized, so everyone was in the other cell. For me, because I'm a juvenile, they didn't put me in the cell at first, but handcuffed me in the passage between the cells. Later they put me in the cell. The stench was like tear-gas.
>
> The cell was tiny, and it was full of feces, bugs, and garbage. I slept on a piece of cardboard on the floor. It was like sleeping in a toilet. And there was an adult, an alleged murderer, right next to me in the cell. At one point I complained about the stench, and the police said it was their job to keep me in the cell, because in the passage I might escape, and they would get in trouble.
>
> When they transferred me to the lockup at Castleton, it was wonderful, by comparison. I had more freedom and space. The only problem was that they put me in a cell with three other juveniles, including a twelve-year-old who tried to hang himself. He was a case of larceny, but they also said he was uncontrollable, so he was in the lockup. But he didn't seem uncontrollable to me, just unhappy. He had a very close bond with his mother, and he missed her. When he tried to hang himself I had to call for the police to lock him down.

When I first was arrested the police were calm and nice. This was, first, because I turned myself in, and second, because I [cooperated]. The investigator was okay. He said I was the only person he ever arrested he didn't have to beat.

Some police were nice; some had attitudes. I guess they're under pressure, too, and sometimes they behave in ways that are bad. I've seen them beat people. I never got beaten. But one time, after they transferred me, they let me out of the jeep, and I thought they were going to take me inside. But a big policeman I didn't know came to me and pulled out his gun and pointed it at my head, and said "This is it!" to me. I was so frightened, it brought tears to my eyes and I felt it emotionally. I thought I would die. I thought, is this how they treat people?

Another policeman told him to leave me alone, and said it was just a joke. But I didn't think it was funny.

Children suffer in police lockups in part because no one Jamaican agency takes responsibility for their welfare. The police, the Children's Services Division, the Correctional Services Department, and the court system all sought to disclaim all responsibility for the plight of children in police lockups.

Police officers told us repeatedly that they did not wish to have responsibility for remand prisoners of any age, since their lockups were designed for only a few short-term prisoners, and not for hundreds of long-term detainees. Despite this, they said, judges keep remanding pretrial prisoners rather than granting them bail, and since space is short in places of safety and remand centers, there's simply nowhere to put prisoners except police lockups. Many senior police officials also told us candidly that the police lacked the training to deal with long-term detainees or juveniles. The police insisted, however, that altering the training given to police or upgrading the lockups was not within their power, for resource reasons, and that these decisions had to be made on the ministerial level.

The Correctional Services Department also disclaimed all responsibility, saying that they were only supposed to hold post-conviction prisoners, and that they currently hold a small number of juveniles on remand only as an interim measure. Senior Correctional Services officials told us that they had no control over whether children were sent to police lockups, or over the conditions in those lockups.

Similarly, the top officials in the Children's Services Division of the Ministry of Health told us they can almost always find spaces for children in places of safety, but that police don't always inform them if children are present in the lockups, and they have no capacity or mandate to inspect or monitor lockups. They also told us that they cannot keep particularly uncontrollable children in their facilities, since their facilities are not secure. In practice, they acknowledged that this means that some children thought to be violent or a consistent discipline problem have no place to go other than lockups.

Finally, the court system disclaims responsibility. The law requires that many children be remanded in custody, either because the children need care and protection or because they are suspected of a serious offense. If a child cannot be released because of the severity of the offense or because he or she has no family able to provide care, and if the remand center or the places of safety cannot or will not take a child, the judge must remand a child back to the lockups.

Human Rights Watch researchers watched a number of Family Court hearings, in one of which a judge reluctantly sent a fifteen-year-old boy back to a police lockup. The boy had been in custody for over a year already, and was still awaiting trial; his trial was delayed because of the difficulty in getting police witnesses to appear in court. The boy had spent a period of time in the remand center, but had been sent back to the lockups because the remand center felt that he was a discipline problem. As we watched, the judge told the boy, "It's not right that young boys should be locked up. Whatever you have done, we can't just give up on you. It's wrong. But there is nothing I can do—I have to send you back [to the lockup] until your trial."

Since each agency that deals in any way with detained children disclaims responsibility for what goes on in the lockups, nothing changes, and decisions are made in a leadership and policy vacuum. No one agency is able entirely to solve the problem of children in lockups, and, too much of the time, this becomes an excuse for each agency to continue to do nothing at all.

For the abuses to be checked, major policy changes must be made at the Jamaican ministerial and parliamentary levels. And in the meantime, all of the relevant agencies need to begin to take responsibility for those aspects of the problem that are within their control, and to collaborate to solve those problems that come about because of poor coordination and communication.

This report is based upon research conducted in Jamaica between August 28 and September 5, 1998. The Human Rights Watch research team visited six police lockups (Spanishtown, Kingston Central, Gun Court, Ewarton, Matilda's Corner, and Portmore). In the first four, our researchers interviewed prisoners; in the latter two, no prisoners were present (at Matilda's Corner, the eight detained children had all been transferred during the day of our visit; at Portmore, the cells were being renovated and no prisoners were yet held). We also sought to visit the lockup at Halfway Tree, whose conditions were reportedly among the most egregious, but although we had previously arranged the visit through the commissioner of police, we were informed upon arrival that we would not be permitted either to tour the cells or interview prisoners. In the lockups, we interviewed about fifteen children between the ages of thirteen and sixteen, along with about the same number of seventeen-year-olds and several adult prisoners. All of the children interviewed in the lockups were male.

Human Rights Watch also visited a "children's home" for girls (a long-term institutional care facility) and two "places of safety" (one for boys and one for girls). All these facilities were run by the Children's Services Division. Finally, we visited Jamaica's only juvenile remand center, run by the Correctional Services Department. In these facilities, we interviewed sixteen children who had previously been held in police lockups for periods ranging from a few days to (in the majority of cases) several weeks or months. The children we interviewed in these facilities ranged in age from twelve to sixteen, and included four girls.

In the children's home and in both of the places of safety, staff respected our request that we be allowed to interview children privately. In both the Juvenile Remand Center and the lockups, however, police officers and facility staff refused to authorize us to interview children privately, although some confidential conversations with children and young adults were in fact possible.

In this report, the names of all children interviewed have been changed to protect the children's privacy.

In addition to visits to places in which children were detained, Human Rights Watch researchers conducted background interviews with ministers, attorneys, representatives of nongovernmental organizations (NGOs), police officers, judges, and social workers. We also interviewed several high-ranking government officials, including the Commissioner of Police, the Commissioner of Correctional Services, and the Director of Children's Services.

II. RECOMMENDATIONS

To the Government of Jamaica

Legal Reform:

* Ensure that Jamaican law conforms to international standards for the treatment of children, and in particular, that the Juveniles Act (as amended) and the Legal Aid Act of 1997 comply with international human rights law. Work to bring Jamaica's juvenile justice system into conformity with the international guidelines expressed in the U.N. Standard Minimum Rules for the Administration of Juvenile Justice (the Beijing Rules). A comprehensive Child Protection Act is currently being drafted to bring Jamaican law into conformity with international standards; this Act should be finalized and implemented.

Police Detention of Children:

* Immediately end the practice of detaining children in police lockup cells.

* If children continue to be held in police lockups, ensure that they at no time share cells with adult detainees.

* If children continue to be detained in police lockups, or if temporary police custody is unavoidable, children should under no circumstances be detained overnight.

* As a step towards ending the practice of detaining children in police lockups, enact measures to minimize the amount of police involvement with children. Police should not bear long-term responsibility for juveniles.

* As a step towards ending the practice of detaining children in police lockups, require police officers to notify Correctional Services and Children's Services immediately upon apprehending a criminally accused child or taking custody of a child "in need of care and protection."

* As a step towards compliance, require superintendents in charge of Jamaica's police lockups to permit unqualified access upon request by an independent monitoring agency empowered to inspect the facilities periodically to ascertain whether children are being improperly detained. Justices of the Peace, Jamaica's parliamentary ombudsman, or other

agents of comparable independence and community status, could be employed to serve in this regard.

- Establish institutions and procedures to expedite the investigation and punishment of police officers who commit abuses, and take immediate steps to eliminate police brutality, including enforcing stringent guidelines to govern the treatment of pretrial detainees.

- Maintain adequate records regarding the arrest and detention of children, including, inter alia, each child's name, date of birth, alleged crime or reason for detention, existing family members or guardians, place(s) of detention, the dates and reasons for transfer between institutions, and court history.

- The Ministry of Justice and National Security should order an immediate review of all children in police custody or remand centers with an eye toward promptly releasing those who pose no threat to public safety.

Children in Detention and Custody, Generally:
- Ensure that in all facilities housing or detaining children, staff are trained in the special needs of children, and treat children with respect and dignity.

- Protect children in state detention or custody from assaults and all forms of cruel, humiliating or degrading treatment by police, staff, or other detainees.

- Ensure that all institutions in which children are housed provide a safe and healthy environment for children. Correct any health code violations promptly.

- Provide medical evaluations and treatment for all children in state custody; maintain records of health status and medication given.

- In all facilities in which children are housed or detained, provide adequate programming and educational instruction to ensure that children are not spending their time without any activity. The purpose of programming and education is to prepare children for successful reintegration into society.

- Establish a clear prohibition on the use of corporal punishment in police lockups, schools, places of safety, children's homes and the Juvenile Remand Center.

- Establish grievance procedures for children in all institutions.

- Ask the U.N. Crime Prevention and Criminal Justice Centre in Vienna for technical assistance to ameliorate the treatment of children in the justice system.

- If existing places of safety, children's homes and remand centers are inadequate to house the number of children requiring short or longer-term custody or care, develop additional placements that are appropriate for children.

- In particular, continue to explore alternatives to institutionalization, and expand community-based parole and placement options for children, particularly those apprehended for status offenses and non-violent crimes.

Access of Children to Counsel and to the Courts:

- Fully implement the Legal Aid Act of 1997, and ensure that all detained children are represented by attorneys, at government expense if a child is unable to afford an attorney.

- Provide children with regular access to their attorneys, in person or by telephone.

- Ensure that private attorneys assigned to provide legal aid to children accused of offenses discharge their responsibilities professionally and provide representation that safeguards the best interests of the child. Lawyers who mismanage, neglect or negligently handle the juvenile criminal cases they have been assigned should be subject to sanctions by the General Legal Counsel.

- The Legal Aid Clinic at Norman Manley Law School should be expanded in order to alleviate some of the caseload currently borne by private attorneys and the legal aid offices of Montego Bay and Kingston.

- Enforce the right of children to a speedy trial and, in particular, cease remanding children into police custody when trials are delayed because of the absence of police witnesses or other evidentiary factors beyond the child's control. Should police or other witnesses fail to appear as required, children should not be punished by further remands and indefinite detention.

- Judges in the family and juvenile courts should ensure that, when the remand of a child becomes strictly necessary, the child will be held at an appropriate institution for children. Under no circumstances should this determination of an "appropriate institution" be delegated to the Jamaican constabulary.

- Take steps to reduce the persistent backlog in the juvenile and family courts.

Other Recommendations to the Jamaican Government:

- The current Ministry of Justice and National Security was consolidated several years ago from the previously distinct Ministries of Justice and National Security. The government should consider separating the ministries again, because of the divergent, and at times contrary, prerogatives pursued by each.

- Institute programs to reduce juvenile crime and to improve relations between local communities and the Jamaican constabulary.

- Establish an interagency children's board to facilitate communication and coordination between and among the Jamaican Constabulary, Children's Services and Correctional Services.

To the Jamaican Constabulary

- Enforce the existing policy that requires police officers, whenever they detain a child temporarily in custody, to submit a written report immediately describing the exigent circumstances that necessitate this measure.

- Instruct officers to immediately transfer children "in need of care and protection" to places of safety.

- Ensure that children are not interrogated in the absence of lawyers.

- Improve communications facilities at remote and rural police lockups. Ensure that each, at a minimum, maintains some means of immediately contacting Children's Services.

- Provide training to police, both new recruits and current officers, that emphasizes the distinctive procedures and attitudes that should inform their treatment of children, both those in conflict with the law and those deemed "in need of care and protection."

- Prominently post rules relating to children in all police stations and ensure that all officers comply with them.

- Immediately institute measures to improve conditions in police lockups, including but not limited to:
    - improving cell ventilation to ensure an adequate flow of fresh air;
    - ensuring that cells are properly maintained and are clean and dry;
    - ensuring that detainees receive plentiful clean water and fresh food adequate to their nutritional needs;
    - providing soap, bedding material, and other basic sanitary necessities;
    - ensuring that all prisoners receive at least one hour of exercise each day;
    - initiating programs of education for longer-term detainees;
    - ensuring that toilets and other sanitary facilities in lockups are kept clean and in good working order,
    - ensuring that children are permitted to use the toilets as needed;
    - ensuring that detainees receive adequate medical care and that a doctor visits regularly.

To the Department of Children's Services
- Assume responsibility for ensuring that police lockups are regularly inspected to ascertain whether children have been improperly detained. If necessary, enlist the assistance of well-respected and independent institutions, whether public, such as Justices of the Peace, or private, such as local church groups and community leaders.

- Keep the police apprised of current vacancies at children's homes and places of safety.

- Establish a twenty-four-hour hotline to facilitate immediate communication between police and children's services whenever a child has been apprehended or been found in need of care and protection.

- Cooperate with church groups and nongovernmental organizations to encourage greater community awareness of and assistance for children in need.

- Improve intake procedures at places of safety and children's homes, and in particular, inquire into the child's prior history in state institutions and the possible existence of relatives or guardians responsible for the child's well-being.

To the Department of Correctional Services
- Transfer all remanded children who do not require detention in a maximum security facility to places of safety and children's homes. The Juvenile Remand Center should be reserved strictly for children deemed dangerous to themselves or others.

- Regularly provide Children's Services with information concerning the number of vacancies available in the Juvenile Remand Center and the presence of children who may not (or no longer) require maximum security detention.

To the United Nations
- The U.N. Committee on the Rights of the Child should reexamine the treatment of children in police custody and institutions and make its best efforts to persuade Jamaica to ensure safe, healthy, and non-abusive treatment of children in the justice system.

- UNICEF should provide assistance to the government of Jamaica to improve the treatment of children in the justice system.

- The World Health Organization should investigate the conditions in which children are detained in unhealthy lockups.

• The U.N. Crime Prevention and Criminal Justice Center should give technical assistance to the Jamaican government to correct existing problems in the juvenile justice system.

• The U.N. Special Rapporteur on Torture and Other Cruel, Inhuman or Degrading Treatment or Punishment should visit Jamaica and investigate the treatment of children in the justice system.

To Donor Governments:
Donor governments should earmark assistance for:

• improving conditions in police lockups, remand centers, and other facilities for children;

• ending delays in handling cases of children in Jamaican courts;

• training police, care-givers and other staff members who deal with children in the justice system.

III. BACKGROUND

In many ways we have regressed as a nation. Poverty is on the increase, the educational system can't keep up, and more and more kids have no stable adult presence in their lives. In poor neighborhoods, the relations with police are tension-filled, and there are all sorts of allegations of police brutality. . . . Some communities are virtual war zones. And there aren't enough children's services. . . . Many of us middle class people are not even aware of how life has changed for many people in our country, how life is for poor children. There's a lack of care and concern. It's a breakdown of community. . . . For some people, ignorance is bliss. They don't want to know. For many people, these are nobody's children.

— The Reverend Norbert Stephens[4]

This section surveys the principal domestic and international legal standards governing Jamaica's treatment of children,[5] and it describes the social, economic, cultural, and political background against which these laws operate.

Jamaica's domestic law and international legal commitments appear to guarantee children some of the rights required by international standards for the protection of minors. Yet social, economic, and political factors—rooted in Jamaican history and the influence of contemporary trends—often combine to subvert many of these standards. The socioeconomic conditions under which Jamaica's legal obligations must be implemented, coupled with escalating societal unrest over juvenile crime, have created circumstances in which children's rights become a low priority—and the legal framework that in theory protects children often breaks down in practice.

---

[4]Human Rights Watch interview with community activist Associate Pastor Norbert Stephens, United Meadowbrook Church, Kingston, Jamaica, August 31, 1998.

[5]In this report, the word "children" refers to anyone under the age of eighteen. Human Rights Watch follows the U.N. Convention on the Rights of the Child in defining as a child "every human being under the age of eighteen unless, under the law applicable to the child, majority is obtained earlier." Convention on the Rights of the Child, G.A. res. 44/25, annex 44 U.N. GAOR Supp. (No 49), at 167, U.N. Doc. A/4/49 (1989), Art. 1. The full text of the Convention on the Rights of the Child appears in the Appendix.

A Context of Rising Juvenile Crime

While politics has been an abiding source of division and, at times, large-scale violence in Jamaican society,[6] many Human Rights Watch interviewees told us that political affiliations in Jamaica today reflect a sense of personal identification and historical loyalty more than any major ideological differences.[7] From the mid-twentieth century to the early 1980s, political patronage at times consisted in certain corrupt politicians distributing guns, material goods and other favors to establish spheres of influence and gain votes.[8] Today, inherited loyalties to one party or the other often remain in many Jamaican communities, even though the original reasons for loyalty to a particular party may no longer exist.[9]

---

[6]See generally, "In Politics: Jamaica's Prime Ministers Seeks An End to violence", *Los Angeles Sentinel*, September 12, 1996. "Political tribalism is a violent fact of life in Jamaica, particularly among groups called 'political garrisons'. . . .Rival factions have been known to kill and maim their opponents, destroying property in the name of their political parties—despite disclaimers by party leaders." Acknowledging this problem in 1996, Prime Minister P.J. Patterson established a twelve-member national committee to address what he called the "'cancer in our midst'" and " to tackle the daunting problem of Jamaica's political violence." Ibid.

[7]See, for example, Julia Preston, "Limbo Lingo Gives Politics a Lilt," *Washington Post,* February 14, 1989. "Manley's National People's Party and Edward Seaga's Jamaica Labor Party are the two great clans of the Jamaican family. Especially among the poor majority, known as the 'sufferers,' the bonds that hold each side together are only partly related to issues. Another tie comes from five decades of traditions and patronage passed down since both parties were founded in the 1930s."

[8]Florence O'Connor, Jamaican community activist and former head of the Jamaica Council for Human Rights, noted that in the past, "[p]oliticians imported guns into Jamaica, but as they lost the ability to meet the economic needs of those to whom they supplied the guns, trade in hard drugs took over . . . ." Ibid.

[9]Human Rights Watch interview with Associate Pastor Stephens, August 31, 1998. See also, Kenneth Blackman, "Jamaica: Drugs, Politics and Poverty Blamed for Wave of Violence," Inter Press Service, March 6, 1992. "Tribalism, the visceral adherence to a political party based on emotional commitment and irrespective of any policy-related or ideological considerations, is one of the main features of Jamaican politics"; and "Economy Drags Jamaica Leader Down in Polls Politics: Apathy Runs High Among Voters," *Los Angeles Times*, March 15, 1992. For a discussion of recent Jamaican political allegiances, see generally Caroline Moser and Jeremy Holland, *Urban Poverty and Violence in Jamaica* (Washington, D.C.: The International Bank for Reconstruction and Development/The World Bank, 1997), and Centre for Population, Community and Social Change, *They Cry 'Respect!': Urban Violence and Poverty in Jamaica* (Kingston: Centre for Population,

Since the mid-1970s, Jamaica's economy has suffered significant decline. The demand for bauxite slowed in the late-1960s and an increase in crime and violence caused lasting damage to Jamaica's tourist industry. This decline continues. In the words of Jamaican community activist Father Richard Albert, "After more than thirty-five years of independence, things have gotten worse . . . . banks are closing, and the middle class is being wiped out."[10]

Jamaica's Gross Domestic Product (GDP) growth rate fell from 1.4 percent in 1993 to –2.4 percent in 1997.[11] Economic decline, in turn, has exacerbated Jamaica's escalating crime rates. Although the overall incidence of reported crimes fell by 10 percent in 1997, the 1990s have witnessed an average annual increase of 3.2 percent, and the murder rate has continued to rise by approximately 11 percent per year.[12] The origins of Jamaica's consistent problem with urban violence, while complex, appear to have originated in significant part from in its turbulent political history.

Political Violence and the Emergence of Youth Gangs

According to a recent World Bank report on urban poverty and violence in Jamaica, partisan political violence has been "a constant feature of Jamaican party politics, from the first elections in 1944."[13] While initially partisan violence involved "sticks-and-stones clashes"[14] intended to intimidate voters, the polarization of Jamaica's urban communities became increasingly warlike. According to many observers of the Jamaican political scene, however, political patronage in the form of weapons "handouts" has declined recently, leading to what some commentators see as the "steady reduction of political violence in the late 1980s and its virtual cessation by the early '90s."[15] Instead, the gangs that arose out of party violence have grown increasingly independent of their political

Community and Social Change, 1996).

[10]Human Rights Watch interview with Father Richard Albert, Kingston, Jamaica, August 30, 1998.

[11] Planning Institute of Jamaica, *Economic and Social Survey Jamaica 1997* (Kingston: Planning Institute of Jamaica, 1998), p. iii.

[12]Ibid., p. viii.

[13]Moser and Holland, *Urban Poverty and Violence in Jamaica*, p. 2.

[14]Ibid., p. 13.

[15]Centre for Population, *They Cry 'Respect!': Urban Violence and Poverty in Jamaica*, p. 8.

origins.[16] Local "dons" now stake out spheres of control within poor urban communities, and clashes over territory, status, and control (of the drug trade, for instance) generate fighting between the various gangs.

This has coincided with a dramatic increase in youth crime. As the World Bank study observed, "A decade ago gangs were formed by young adults. Today's gangs comprised youths aged twelve to fifteen, and every youth had access to a gun if he wished."[17] In Jamaica, where approximately forty percent of the population consists of children aged eleven to seventeen,[18] this trend is widely perceived as a serious problem by the general populace and has encouraged a "tough-on-crime" political atmosphere[19] that devalues concern for the human rights of children

---

[16]Jamaican sociologist and pollster Carl Stone described this transition vividly, observing that "[i]nitially, they were petty criminals fighting over control of territory . . . . After they were discovered by political parties, they were made into mercenary adjuncts to JLP and PNP party campaign machinery, helping to keep political territory safe. Then the gangs became disconnected from the parties while retaining their political loyalties and emerged as managers of whole communities, which they controlled by the gun. In the final phase, the gangs have got into the drug business as powerful entrepreneurs in their own right, selling and dispensing hard drugs, buying the loyalty of renegade policeman and holding whole communities under their power." Don Bohning, "Gang Violence Surges in Ghettos of Jamaica's Capital: Problem Transcends Political Origins as Groups Pursue Drug Trade, Seek to Show Independence," *Dallas Morning News*, March 1, 1992. *See also*, Kenneth Freed, "Drugs Have Replaced Politics as Fuel for Jamaica Violence," *Star Tribune*, November 29, 1992. "The gangs were the creations of the country's two major parties and they used violence mostly to sway voters and promote political programs. That has largely changed. While the gangs still define themselves in terms of parties and still control patronage and other political spoils, most of the their work and money comes from the cocaine trade."

[17]Moser and Holland, *Urban Poverty and Violence in Jamaica*, p. 15.

[18]Human Rights Watch interview with Ambassador Marjorie Taylor, Minister of State and Special Envoy on Children, Ministry of Health, Kingston, Jamaica, August 31, 1998. According to a 1996 survey, 35.2 percent of Jamaica's population is under the age of fifteen and approximately 26.3 percent falls between the ages of fifteen and twenty-nine. The Planning Institute of Jamaica and the Statistical Institute of Jamaica, *Jamaica Survey of Living Conditions 1996* (Kingston: The Planning Institute of Jamaica and the Statistical Institute of Jamaica, 1997), p. 1.

[19]This atmosphere helps explain the motivation behind Jamaica's decision on October 23, 1997, to denounce the First Optional Protocol to the International Covenant on Civil and Political Rights (ICCPR)—the first such denunciation since the protocol took effect. The First Optional Protocol permits the U.N. Human Rights Committee to examine communications from individuals claiming to be victims of violations of the rights set forth in the ICCPR. Jamaica's denunciation took effect on January 23, 1998.

accused of offenses. As Lloyd Barnett of the Jamaica Council for Human Rights notes wryly, "The public are more concerned with their own safety than with [programs that emphasize] prevention or with helping detained kids."[20]

Relations Between the Urban Poor and Jamaica's Constabulary

The emerging phenomenon of youth gangs has exacerbated the already tense relationship between the Jamaican Constabulary and local urban communities. Gangs undoubtedly contribute to urban violence—yet in many poor communities, residents may come to perceive their local "dons" as protectors, providing security, stability, and order that the police fail to offer. A recent report by the Centre for Population, Community and Social Change describes this phenomenon:

> Whatever the acts of terror against a rival community, or the illegal acts against outside businesses or individuals, *the rule was not to terrorize the people of your own community* . . . . This made for a perceived and appreciated intra-community safety and order, even in the midst of the war between communities. Often as a result, the dons and other lesser Robin Hood gunmen, who distributed to the poor what they robbed from the rich, were protected by the community from the strict arm of the law.[21]

Consequently, local residents at times refuse to cooperate with police inquiries into violence between rival gangs, preferring to trust and rely upon those who are rooted in the community, rather than the police, who may be viewed as outsiders—and, indeed, even as oppressors—as they seek to stamp out many of the illegal or quasi-legal activities through which some poor urban communities maintain their economic viability.[22] This attitude, in turn, provokes the police to

---

[20]Human Rights Watch interview with Lloyd Barnett, Kingston, Jamaica, August 28, 1998.

[21]Centre for Population, *They Cry 'Respect!': Urban Violence and Poverty in Jamaica*, p.7 (emphasis in original).

[22]Commissioner Forbes suggested that this tension is rooted in the role of the police during Jamaica's colonial period, when many Jamaicans viewed police as the enforcers of the interests of the landed aristocracy rather than protectors of the public. Human Rights Watch interview with Francis Forbes, Commissioner of Police, Kingston, Jamaica, August 28, 1998.

resort to further force in dealing with recalcitrant communities, escalating the mutual distrust and hostility between Jamaican police and civilians.

Human rights abuses by the Jamaican police have been well documented and publicized.[23] Many human rights abuses perpetrated by the Jamaican police—including, for instance, summary executions disguised as killings in shoot-outs and unprovoked brutality towards vagrants and street children—stem from what the U.S. Department of State terms a "long-standing antipathy between the security forces and certain communities, especially the urban poor."[24]

While both current Police Commissioner Francis Forbes and his predecessor, Commissioner McMillian, have made efforts to ameliorate these tensions by professionalizing the force, many urban poor, particularly the young, continue to view the police with suspicion and often with outright hostility. And as Carl Rattray, the President of the Jamaican Court of Appeals, observed, "If the community views the police as the enemy, policing becomes very difficult, leading to worsening relations . . . when there's disturbances in the area, the police will often just sweep everyone up."[25]

Agencies With Responsibility for Children

The Role of the Police

Among those government agencies that share responsibility for children, the police constitute both the most likely "first contact," as well as an agency empowered to exercise broad discretion at a crucial juncture in the series of events affecting children's welfare. Police who apprehend a child on suspicion of criminal activity—or who assume custody, whether by request or by warrant, over a child "in need of care and protection"—have the independent authority to place a child in a "place of safety," to detain him or her *temporarily* in a lockup should the child be deemed dangerous, or to return the child to his or her parent or guardian.

Jamaican law states that no child should be held for over twenty-four hours in police custody. If exceptions are made, Police Commissioner Forbes explained, officers who detain children for a period beyond twenty-four hours must

---

[23] *See, for example*, U.S. Department of State, Bureau of Democracy, Human Rights and Labor, *Jamaica Country Report on Human Rights Practices for 1997* (Washington, D.C.: U.S. Department of State, 1998).

[24] Ibid.

[25] Human Rights Watch interview with Justice Carl Rattray, President, Court of Appeal and former Minister of Justice, Kingston, Jamaica, September 3, 1998.

submit a written report explaining the extenuating circumstances that necessitate this measure.[26]

Nevertheless, in practice, Human Rights Watch found that police often detain children for longer periods, sometimes for articulable reasons (e.g., because transferring a child to an alternative facility would require unavailable transportation or because they believe other facilities to be full) but often simply because police feel justified in exercising their discretion to detain certain juvenile offenders in lockups as an unauthorized punitive measure.[27]

The Children's Services Division

An officer who apprehends a child has the responsibility to locate an immediate placement for that child in a facility run by the Children's Services Division, an independent agency within the jurisdiction of the Ministry of Health. The Children's Services Division handles children in need of care and protection (i.e., children abused, neglected, or abandoned), children accused of the commission of a criminal offense (with the exception of those deemed by the court system to be so violent or dangerous as to warrant continuing police custody), and children whose parents surrender them as "uncontrollable." If, after contacting all the relevant facilities in search of an appropriate placement for an apprehended child, a police officer finds that no space is available, he or she is supposed to immediately notify the Children's Services Division, which will then locate alternative temporary placements for the child.

Depending upon the needs of the child, Children's Services can facilitate court proceedings, provide temporary shelter for a child in a "place of safety" (pending trial or long-term placement), communicate with the child's parents or guardians or provide long-term supervision for the child through foster care, adoption or placement of the child in a "children's home."

Although Children's Services is the central agency responsible for children's welfare, they rely heavily on police information and cooperation to render services to children in need. Should the police fail to inform the agency of a child apprehended or "in need of care and protection," Children's Services lacks a monitoring mechanism for discovering the existence of a child in need of its services.

---

[26]Human Rights Watch interview with Commissioner Forbes, August 28, 1998.

[27]Human Rights Watch interview with Leo Equiano, Director, Kingston Legal Aid Clinic, Kingston, Jamaica, September 1, 1998.

The Department of Correctional Services

The final agency that bears some responsibility for children's welfare under Jamaica's current system is the Department of Correctional Services, which lies within the jurisdiction of the Ministry of Justice and National Security.[28] According to the formal division of responsibility among Jamaica's governmental agencies, Correctional Services bears responsibility only for convicted children. It administers two "approved schools" or "juvenile correctional centers" for boys (Rio Cobre and Hilltop), and one similar institution for girls (Armadale). After a judge enters a correctional order, Correctional Services assumes custody of the child and places him or her in one of these maximum security facilities. Children in these institutions receive some educational and vocational training, and provision is made for their exercise and recreation.

Correctional Services also administers Jamaica's sole "juvenile remand center," a maximum security detention facility used to hold children accused of more serious crimes pending trial. Although Correctional Services, as its representatives repeatedly emphasized, is not "responsible for remands; remands are strictly for Children's Services,"[29] it administers the juvenile remand center because it maintains the necessary staff and resources to adequately handle children who must be detained in a maximum security facility. Though the Juvenile Remand Center is not intended as a center for the long-term placement of children, in practice, the consistent backlog of cases in family and juvenile court often keeps children at the Remand Center for over a year.

Relevant Legal Standards

International Legal Standards

Under international law, children enjoy rights and protections derived not only from human rights treaties that pertain generally to all individuals, such as the International Covenant on Civil and Political Rights (ICCPR),[30] but also from

---

[28]Several years ago, the Ministries of National Security and Justice, formerly separate ministries, were consolidated. Justice Carl Rattray, former minister of justice, noted that the merger of National Security and Justice creates internal conflict, since the demands of justice sometimes conflict with an emphasis on security, particularly in a country permeated by a "tough on crime" political rhetoric. Human Rights Watch interview with Justice Carl Rattray, September 3, 1998.

[29]Human Rights Watch interview with June Jarret, Director, Juvenile Institutions, St. Andrews Juvenile Remand Center, Kingston, Jamaica, September 3, 1998.

[30]G.A. Res. A/2200/XXI, December 16, 1966; entered into force March 23, 1976.

treaties and internationally acknowledged guidelines designed expressly to address the special needs of children. These include the U.N. Standard Minimum Rules for the Administration of Juvenile Justice (Beijing Rules),[31] the U.N. Rules for the Protection of Juveniles Deprived of Their Liberty (U.N. Rules),[32] the United Nations Guidelines for the Prevention of Juvenile Delinquency (Riyadh Guidelines)[33] and, most critically, the Convention on the Rights of the Child (CRC).[34] Moreover, children in detention, like all detained persons, should be treated in a manner that conforms to the Standard Minimum Rules for the Treatment of Prisoners (Standard Minimum Rules).[35]

The CRC presumptively defines a juvenile as an individual under the age of eighteen,[36] and it sets forth several broad categories of rights belonging to children. Jamaica signed and ratified the CRC on, respectively, January 26, 1990, and May 14, 1991. The Beijing Rules, Riyadh, Guidelines and U.N. Rules provide additional authoritative guidance that informs the practical content of the legally binding framework established by the CRC. They also provide explicit standards to guide states' treatment of juveniles who come into conflict with the law. Together, these instruments afford children, inter alia, the following general categories of rights and protections:

Protection from Violence, Injury, and Neglect

Under the CRC, states undertake to shield children from ill-treatment, including protection from violence, injury, sexual abuse, and neglect.[37] With due regard for parental rights, this includes establishing alternative institutions for children who lack a stable and healthy family environment.[38] All decisions concerning removal of children from their parents or guardians must be made with regard for the best interests of the child under the circumstances.[39]

---

[31]G.A. Res. 40/33, November 29, 1985.
[32]G.A. Res. 45/113, April 2, 1991.
[33]G.A. Res. 45/112, March 28, 1991.
[34]G.A. Res. 44/25, November 20, 1989.
[35]ECOSOC Res. 663 C (XXIV), July 31, 1957, and 2076 (LXII), May 13, 1977.
[36]CRC., Art. 1.
[37]Ibid, Art. 19, 34.
[38]Ibid., Art. 20.
[39]Ibid, Art. 3(1); Riyadh Guidelines, Art. 46.

Access to Health Care, Education, and Recreation

States recognize that children possess the right to a "a standard of living adequate for the child's physical, mental, spiritual, moral, and social development,"[40] and they undertake, as necessary, to implement measures ensuring children health care, education, and recreation.[41] The U.N. Rules extend these guarantees to children who come into conflict with the law.[42] The CRC also requires that special care be afforded to mentally or physically disabled children.[43]

Rights of Children Accused of Criminal Offenses

Article 40 of the CRC sets forth minimum standards[44] governing states' treatment of children accused of criminal offenses. These include, among others:

- The right to be presumed innocent until proven guilty.

- The right to be informed promptly of the criminal charges alleged against them.

- The right to trial without delay by a competent and impartial tribunal.

- The right to legal counsel and, if necessary, to an interpreter.

The Beijing Rules reaffirm these "basic procedural safeguards"[45] but additionally set forth special measures concerning the investigation and prosecution of juvenile cases, as well as their adjudication and disposition:

- Officials apprehending juveniles on suspicion of criminal conduct should immediately notify the child's parents or guardians and a judge or other authoritative body who "shall, without delay, consider the issue of release."[46]

---

[40]CRC, Art. 27.
[41]Ibid., Arts. 24, 27- 29, 31.
[42]U.N. Rules, Arts. 38-40, 47, 49-55.
[43]CRC, Art. 23.
[44]See Ibid, Art. 40(2).
[45]Beijing Rules, Art. 7
[46]Ibid., Art. 10.

- Officers who deal frequently with juvenile crime should be specially trained to handle the distinctive needs of children in conflict with the law.[47]

- Neither corporal punishment nor, in those states that maintain it, capital punishment should be imposed on children, notwithstanding the nature of the crime.[48]

- Lastly, states must make available a broad variety of measures—including, but not limited to, community service orders, foster care, group counseling, restitution, and probation—that afford the judiciary maximal "flexibility so as to avoid institutionalization to the greatest extent possible."[49]

Rights of Children in Detention

The CRC proscribes the arbitrary detention of children and dictates that arrest, detention, and imprisonment of children "shall be used only as a measure of last resort and for the shortest appropriate period of time."[50] This principle, paramount among legal guidelines for the treatment of children, also features emphatically in the Beijing Rules, the Riyadh Guidelines, and the U.N. Rules,[51] reflecting broad international consensus that incarcerating children is rarely appropriate. When the detention of children in conflict with the law becomes unavoidable, the CRC and related international guidelines delineate strict standards to which states must adhere:

- Juveniles must be detained separately from adults, either in a separate institution or in a segregated area of an institution that also holds adult detainees.[52]

- Children awaiting trial must be separated from convicted children.[53]

---

[47]Ibid., Art. 12.1
[48]Ibid, Arts. 17.2, 17.3.
[49]Ibid., Art. 18.1
[50]CRC, Art. 37.
[51]Beijing Rules, Art. 19(1); Riyadh Guidelines, Art. 46; U.N. Rules, Art. 1.
[52]Beijing Rules, Art. 13.4; CRC, Art. 37(c); U.N. Rules, Art. 29.
[53]U.N. Rules, Art. 17.

- Upon admission, the authorities shall conduct an interview with the child and prepare a "psychological and social report identifying any factors relevant to the specific type and level of care and programme required."[54]

- Detention facilities must provide clean sleeping accommodations and sanitary facilities adequate to their health and privacy needs.[55]

- Children in custody must be provided with education, preferably at an institution away from the detention facility, medical treatment, and a physical environment with adequate provision for recreation and exercise.[56]

- No child in detention shall be subjected to "cruel, inhuman or degrading treatment, including corporal punishment, placement in a dark cell, closed or solitary confinement or any other punishment that may compromise the physical or mental health" of the child.[57]

- The state should provide for unqualified access to juvenile detention facilities by an independent inspection agency not directly affiliated with the detention facility.[58]

- Children enjoy all rights and standards set forth in the Standard Minimum Rules, including those to adequate accommodation, personal hygiene, clothing, food and exercise, as well as to protection from disciplinary measures that abrogate the guidelines promulgated by the Standard Minimum Rules[59] and access to an independent complaints mechanism.[60]

---

[54]Ibid, Art. 27.
[55]Ibid, Art. 34.
[56]Ibid, Arts. 38-40, 47, 49.
[57]Ibid, Art. 67. *See also* CRC, Art. 37(a).
[58]U.N. Rules, Art. 72.
[59]*See* Standard Minimum Rules, Arts. 27-32.
[60]Beijing Rules, Art. 13.3; U.N. Rules, Art. 2. *See generally* Standard Minimum Rules.

Domestic Legal Standards

The Jamaican Constitution (1962)

Chapter III of Jamaica's 1962 Constitution affords all Jamaican citizens fundamental human rights and freedoms, including the right to life, freedom from arbitrary arrest and detention, protection from torture and other cruel, inhuman, and degrading treatment, as well as a catalogue of widely shared protections for the criminally accused. Its language closely tracks the Universal Declaration of Human Rights[61] and the International Covenant on Civil and Political Rights.

The Juveniles Act of 1951

"When a tree is old, you can't bend it. You can only bend it when it is young."

> — Sipzroy Bryan, Jamaican Union of Correctional Officers[62]

The Jamaica Juveniles Act of 1951 (Juveniles Act), as amended, constitutes the principal domestic instrument that implements rights recognized by the Convention on the Rights of the Child and related international guidelines. In conformity with Article 4 of the U.N. Rules, the Juveniles Act sets forth a minimum age (twelve years) beneath which no child may be found criminally liable.[63] In addition, the Juveniles Act defines "juvenile," for purposes of criminal responsibility, as a person beneath the age of seventeen.[64]

Consequently, although the "Age of Majority Act" defines a child as any person under the age of eighteen, Jamaica persists in treating seventeen-year-olds accused of criminal offenses as adults; and they may be tried and sentenced accordingly.[65]

---

[61]Universal Declaration of Human Rights, G.A. Res. 217 A (III), December 10, 1948.

[62]Human Rights Watch interview with Sipzroy Bryan, Kingston, Jamaica, August 28, 1998.

[63]Juveniles Act, Sec. 3.

[64]Ibid., Sec. 2.

[65] Caribbean Children's Law Project, 2.2. "A person is of full age and capacity on attaining the age of 18." Law Reform (Age of Majority) Act of 1979.

The Juveniles Act establishes a series of measures designed to address (1) juveniles "in need of care and protection"; and (2) juveniles accused of criminal offenses. Article 11 authorizes judicial officers to issue a warrant permitting constables to remove abused, neglected, or otherwise maltreated children to "places of safety,"[66] where they may be held pending disposition of their case by the court.[67] Constables and other authorized individuals may also bring before the juvenile court children who seek their assistance (e.g., runaways or abused children) and are deemed "in need of care and protection."[68]

When the child's case comes before the court, a justice may either (1) issue an "interim order" remanding the child to a place of safety or to the Juvenile Remand Center for up to thirty days, pending the gathering of further germane information or the location of the child's relations; or (2) issue one of four dispositive orders directing that: (a) the child be sent to a "juvenile correctional center,"[69] (b) the child be committed to the care of a "fit person," whether a relative or not, (c) the child's parent or guardian "take recognizance" of and properly care for the child, or (d) the child be placed under the supervision of a probation officer for a period not to exceed three years.[70]

The court's decision concerning children "in need of care and protection" will, in theory, be informed by the investigation and report of a "children's officer."[71] Moreover, according to several interviewees, children "in need of care and protection" should not be remanded more than two times and should spend no more than a total of ninety days in a place of safety or at the juvenile remand center; the Juveniles Act, however, contains no express provision to this effect.

The Juveniles Act invests the Commissioner of Police with responsibility to ensure that juveniles apprehended on suspicion of criminal activity are not

---

[66] Places of safety are holding facilities of varying levels of security that in theory provide a temporary home for children "in need of care and protection" and for children accused of lesser offenses.

[67] Juveniles Act, Sec. 11.

[68] Ibid, Sec. 13.

[69] An juvenile correctional center is a high security juvenile facility designed for long-term care and rehabilitation of both convicted children and children deemed dangerously uncontrollable. Juvenile correctional centers were formerly known as "approved schools." Human Rights Watch interview with June Jarret, Director of Juvenile Institutions, Kingston, Jamaica, September 2, 1998.

[70] Juveniles Act., Sec. 14.

[71] Jamaica presently maintains, however, only five children's officers. Human Rights Watch interview with Afshan Khan, Communications Consultant, UNICEF, Kingston, Jamaica, September 1, 1998.

detained with adults.[72] It further entrusts "the officer or sub-officer of police in charge of the police station to which he [the juvenile] is brought" with discretion, based on an inquiry into the child's case, either to release the child to an appropriate individual on bail or to detain the child at a place of safety pending his or her court appearance.[73] Thereafter, the court maintains power to remand children into custody, pending the production of witnesses or the procurement of evidence, or, if necessary, to commit the child to a maximum security facility, "including a prison."[74]

Police bear the responsibility for finding a place of safety in which to detain the child pending disposition of the case. Although no provision limits the number of times that a juvenile accused of an offense may be remanded, the Juveniles Act provides that the accused child must appear before the court at least once every thirty days.[75]

At trial, "it shall be the duty of the court to ascertain the defense, if any, of the juvenile"[76] and ultimately, to record a finding based upon the evidence as well as upon germane information submitted by a probation officer assigned to investigate the child's case.

Upon conviction, the court may issue one of eight dispositive orders, including dismissing the case, committing the child to the care of a probation officer[77] or guardian, returning the child to his or her parents, ordering criminal restitution, and sentencing the child to a "juvenile correctional facility." Both children "in need of care and protection" and children convicted of minor offenses may also be committed to the care of a "children's home"[78] at the discretion of the court.

The Juveniles Act prohibits capital punishment for juveniles.[79] Instead of executing juveniles who have committed capital offenses, however, Jamaica detains them under an antiquated law known as the "Governor General's Pleasure,"

---

[72]Juveniles Act, Sec. 17.

[73]Ibid., Sec. 18.

[74]Ibid., Sec. 19(1)-(2).

[75]Ibid., Sec. 24.

[76]Ibid, Sec. 22(8).

[77]Probation officers handle investigations in connection with children accused of criminal offenses; children's officers deal principally with children "in need of care and protection."

[78]Children's homes are long-term foster care centers intended principally for abandoned or neglected children who cannot expect to be returned to their family environment.

[79]Juveniles Act, Sec. 29.

which permits children detained for capital offenses to be held indefinitely at the discretion of the governor-general.[80] Corporal punishment remains legal in schools, in the home and at "places of safety," although approximately one year ago it was prohibited at the Juvenile Remand Center.[81]

Legal Aid

Presently, legal aid in criminal matters is governed by the Poor Prisoners Defense Law of 1961. The judiciary maintains discretion, based upon a means enquiry conducted by probation officers, to grant legal aid to indigent prisoners who face conviction for one of a series of scheduled offenses.[82] These include, for instance, murder, manslaughter, rape, carnal abuse, arson and gun crimes but not theft or simple assault.

Should the court deem it appropriate, the judge will assign a private attorney, who receives a small state subsidy for his services, to represent the defendant. Alternatively, two legal aid clinics exist, one in Montego Bay and one

---

[80]The "Governor General's Pleasure" is modeled after the British practice of detaining certain juvenile offenders indefinitely at "Her Majesty's Pleasure," a phrase derived from the Criminal Lunatics Act of 1800 and the Children's Act of 1908: Where an insane person or a child was deemed to pose a continuing threat to the public despite the expiration of his punitive sentence, he could be detained "at Her Majesty's pleasure" for an indefinite period, i.e, until the Crown determined that the individual no longer posed a threat to the public safety. Several recent decisions by the European Court of Human Rights have affirmed that, in view of the exclusively *preventative* purpose of this practice, juveniles may not be detained as a matter of arbitrary executive discretion; rather, "Article 5 para. 4 (Art. 5-4) [of the European Convention on Human Rights] requires an oral hearing in the context of an adversarial procedure involving legal representation and the possibility of calling and questioning witnesses." *Hussain v. United Kingdom*, 22 Eur. H.R. Rep. 1 (1996). See also *Singh v. United Kingdom*, Case No. 56/1994/503/585, unreported (1996).

[81]Human Rights Watch interview with June Jarret, September 2, 1998. The Juvenile Remand Center is a maximum security holding center for remanded boys—similar to a "place of safety"—that falls under the jurisdiction of Correctional Services rather than Children's Services because Correctional Services maintains trained staff members and resources adequate to handle detainees who may pose greater security risks.

[82]Francis Clift, Michelle Cumbermack, Sonya Gibbs and Lorna King, Caribbean Children's Law Project: *The Law Relating to Children in Barbados, Jamaica, Guyana and Trinidad and Tobago* (London : Hornby, Ackroyd and Levy, [1997], p. 56.

in Kingston, that will provide legal counsel for substantially reduced rates in both scheduled and non-scheduled criminal offenses.[83]

In 1997, the Jamaican parliament passed the Legal Aid Act of 1997. The act has not yet entered into force, but when and if it is implemented, it will change matters significantly, as it disposes of the idea of providing legal aid solely for certain scheduled offenses. Instead, it provides legal aid in criminal matters to "any person who is detained at a police station or in a lockup [or] correctional institution," provided that an application for legal aid is made by or on behalf of the defendant. People who are not in detention may also qualify for legal aid if "it appears to the certifying authority . . . that the person's means are insufficient to enable him to obtain legal services."[84]

The new act therefore expands the range of offenses to which legal aid in criminal matters applies. Additionally, the act would compel police, upon making an arrest, (1) to inform the accused of his or her basic rights, including the right to have access to legal counsel; (2) to make available to defendants a roster of available attorneys; and (3) to facilitate the initial contact between the defendant and an attorney.[85]

Jamaica's 1993 Report to the U.N. Committee on the Rights of the Child

As a state party to the Convention on the Rights of the Child, Jamaica must submit periodic reports to the U.N. Committee on the Rights of Child that describe measures "adopted which give effect to the rights recognized [in the CRC]," as well as "progress made on the enjoyment of those rights."[86]

Following Jamaica's initial submission in 1993, the committee expressed concern regarding three principal areas affecting Jamaica's domestic implementation of the CRC. First, it noted that Jamaica's severe social and economic problems have negatively affected the circumstances of children by, for instance, drastically reducing social services.[87] Second, it expressed concern that

---

[83]Human Rights Watch interview with Leo Equiano, Director, Kingston Legal Aid Clinic, Kingston, Jamaica, September 1, 1998. Mr. Equiano informed us that, for example, whereas a private attorney would charge JA$90,000, legal aid would ask for approximately $15,000.

[84]Legal Aid Act of 1997, Art. 15.

[85]Human Rights Watch interview with Leo Equiano, September 1, 1998.

[86]CRC, Art. 44(1). States party to the CRC undertake to submit an initial report within two years of ratifying and, subsequently, to report at least once every five years.

[87]Committee on the Rights of the Child, Concluding Observations on Jamaica, U.N. Doc. CRC/C/15/Add.32 (Eighth session, 1995), para. 5.

certain "social attitudes, traditions and prejudices" prevalent in Jamaica hampered the effective implementation of the convention.[88]

Perhaps most critically, the committee's report observed that Jamaica lacks "an overall integrated mechanism to monitor the activities designed to promote and protect children's rights," leading to "insufficient coordination between the various governmental departments, as well as between central and regional authorities, in the implementation of the policies to promote and protect the rights of the child . . . ."[89]

While not exhaustive, the U.N. Committee's observations capture several reasons why, despite Jamaica's express international legal obligations and domestic system of implementation, children continue to be detained improperly in adult police lockups.

---

[88]Ibid., para. 6.
[89]Ibid., para. 8.

IV. POLICE LOCKUPS

*"Sometimes juveniles are very violent, more violent than adults.
So at times we have to keep them here."*

> — Superintendent Adams, Spanish Town Station.[90]

"We try to treat [juveniles] well, but some of them don't deserve it."

> — Inspector Broomfield, Gun Court Station[91]

"Adult" Lockups

Spanish Town

Human Rights Watch visited the police lockup at Spanish Town on August 25, 1998. The antiquated facility contains ten cells, each of which measures ten by ten feet and is intended to hold five persons, for a total stated capacity of fifty detainees. On the day of our visit, however, we were informed by Superintendent Adams, the officer in charge at Spanish Town, that it held 138 detainees.[92]

Conditions inside the Spanish Town cells were appalling. Tiny slats in the concrete wall towards the back of each cell provided the only source of light and fresh air. Detainees consequently suffered from a near total absence of light and ventilation, and the level of heat within the cells was unbearable. Together with the severe overcrowding—cells designed for five held thirteen or fourteen prisoners each—these conditions constitute blatant violations of the U.N. and Beijing Rules.

---

[90]Human Rights Watch interview with Superintendent Adams, Spanish Town Police Station, Jamaica, August 29, 1998.

[91]Human Rights Watch interview with Inspector Broomfield, Kingston Central Police Station, Kingston, Jamaica, September 2, 1998.

[92]Human Rights Watch interview with Superintendent Adams, August 29, 1998. A survey written in chalk at the entrance to the cells further classified the detainees into categories such as "convicted," "unconvicted," "in need of care and protection," and "hospital." Moreover, while Superintendent Adams informed us that no juveniles were currently detained at Spanish Town, the same chalked schedule included the category "juveniles," and indicated that ten were currently in detention.

Although some cells contained toilets, most of these were broken, and prisoners told us that often guards refused to let them out to use the filthy but functional toilets located at the end of the cell block. Consequently, detainees were often forced to urinate and defecate in buckets inside the cells, or, in the absence of a bucket, to simply relieve themselves on the floor, exacerbating the already severely substandard sanitary conditions.

The cell floors were filthy, often damp and covered with scattered bits of cardboard and newspaper, which served as the prisoners' only bedding material. Apart from the two or three detainees able to lay claim to the one or two concrete bunk slabs in each cell (none with mattresses or other bedding), prisoners reported that they slept crowded together on the floors. Cockroaches and other insects infest the cells, and many prisoners displayed insect bites.

The police provide medical treatment on an emergency basis only. We interviewed one young man who suffered from chronic asthma, a boy who had oozing sores on his legs and who wept as he spoke to us, and a third man who complained of hearing loss and who had a greenish discharge coming from his ears. None of these individuals had been permitted to see a physician and none had been provided with medication.

The food in Spanish Town, by all accounts, is as poor and scarce as medical care or bedding: many detainees told us that the prison food made them ill, and other prisoners stated flatly that they eat only food that is brought to them by their relatives and friends during visiting hours.

The overwhelming majority of the detainees held in the Spanish Town lockup were unconvicted "remand" prisoners who were awaiting trial. Although some were accused of serious crimes, many were held on suspicion of participation in relatively trivial offenses. Prisoners were not separated by either age or status (convicted or unconvicted); and status offenders and those accused of petty crimes were held in the same cells as men detained for violent crimes. Towards the front of the cell block, three prisoners were held in isolation. According to a guard, they were in personal danger from fellow prisoners,[93] although these individuals told Human Rights Watch that they believed they had been quarantined for contagious illness.[94]

At times, the detainees told us, fights break out among the prisoners, typically over access to scarce material goods, such as cigarettes, food, and money,

---

[93]Human Rights Watch interview with security officer (name withheld), Spanish Town Police Station, August 29, 1998.

[94]Human Rights Watch interviews, Spanish Town Police Station, Jamaica, August 29, 1998.

or over access to sleeping space on the filthy cell floors: overcrowding is so severe that in most cells not everyone can lie down at once. Violence between cellmates was also sometimes motivated by clashing loyalties to political parties, gangs, or neighborhoods. Both guards and detainees told us that guards often resort to violence to break up fighting. Some detainees told us that the police treated them "okay," while others exhibited wounds that they ascribed to unprovoked police violence.

The Spanish Town police lockup is officially for adults only. In our initial interview with superintendent Adams, he stated unequivocally that "[j]uveniles are not kept at Spanish Town,"[95] but he also conceded that seven "juveniles" had recently been "processed" at Spanish Town and sent on to the Ewarton substation. Notwithstanding these statements, a categorization of the prisoners inscribed in chalk at the entrance to the cell block and dated August 25, 1998, indicated that ten juveniles were detained at Spanish Town.

Our interviews at the Spanish Town lockup, though limited in number by difficulties in speaking to children privately, confirmed that children were held there, in violation of both Jamaican law and international standards. We managed to speak to five seventeen-year-olds, two sixteen-year olds, and one boy who was fifteen.

- **Winston**, fifteen, had been detained for approximately six months at the time of our visit, and was held in a cell with eleven adult prisoners.

- **Harold and Jason**, the two sixteen-year-olds, had been detained for several months, and Harold exhibited a large scar on his head that he said was the result of a recent police beating with batons.

Numerous adult prisoners also confirmed that it was not uncommon for fifteen and sixteen-year-olds to be held for several months at a time at Spanish Town.[96]

Kingston Central

On September 3, 1998, Human Rights Watch visited the police lockup at Kingston Central. The detainees had apparently been told that we would visit, and many shouted to us from inside the cells, saying that they needed to talk to us and that conditions were poor.

---

[95]Human Rights Watch interview with Superintendent Adams, August 29, 1998.
[96]Human Rights Watch interviews with detainees (names withheld), Spanish Town Police Station, Jamaica, September 28, 1998.

According to Police Commissioner Francis Forbes, the cells at Kingston Central are, like the cells at Spanish Town, for adults only. But at Kingston Central, too, we found that this rule was honored only in the breach. Upon arriving at Kingston Central, we spoke briefly with Superintendent Bailey and Inspector Cleary, a custody officer at the lockup. Superintendent Bailey informed us that in practice, Kingston Central usually has enough children detained to warrant designating one of the facility's thirty-four cells as a special "juvenile cell."[97]

Of the thirty-four cells, only nine had functioning door locks at the time of our visit. Technically, three to seven prisoners occupy each cell at Kingston Central, depending on the cell's size. But in practice, most prisoners roam freely throughout the hallway due to the defective locks. Kingston Central's maximum stated capacity is ninety-one; on the day we visited, it held one hundred thirty-eight prisoners, of which one hundred thirty were held pending trial (remands), two were convicted, four were apparently detained awaiting transfer elsewhere, and two, according to police, were juveniles. We were told that most of the juveniles had been transferred the day before our visit, but their destination was not identified.[98] Inspector Cleary remarked that, in general, the number of children detained at Kingston Central is typically under ten at any given moment, and their stay is usually of short duration, but he conceded that "sometimes juveniles stay for two to three months."[99]

Conditions within the cellblock were deplorable. At the entrance to the cell block's main gate, a large bin overflowed with trash, and the stench of rotting garbage and urine permeated the air. Two detainees, one of whom was identified as a crack addict and the other as mentally disturbed, were sprawled out on filthy stairs that led up to the second floor of the cellblock, where the cell designated for juveniles was situated.

By contrast to the first floor cells, the "juvenile cell" was comparatively clean: though damp, it contained no trash or sewage.[100] It contained six concrete slab beds. At the time of our visit, two children, both aged sixteen, were in this cell, together with eleven adults ranging in age from eighteen to twenty-four.

---

[97]Human Rights Watch interview with Superintendent Bailey, Kingston Central Police Station, Kingston, Jamaica, September 3, 1998.

[98]Ibid.

[99]Human Rights Watch interview with Inspector Cleary, Kingston Central Police Station, Kingston, Jamaica, September 3, 1998.

[100]We were told by the prisoners, however, that the cells had been hosed down in preparation for our visit, and sewage hosed outside: thus the severe stench right outside the cell block.

• **Travis,** one of the sixteen-year-olds, had been detained since late June 1998. His initial court date was set for August 14, but he was remanded pending a further hearing because the complainant failed to appear.

• **Ryan,** the other sixteen-year-old, had been held for nine months. Although he had appeared at the family court three times during this period, he told us that was never provided with a lawyer, and had been remanded back to the lockup after each court appearance.

Both boys related that the guards serve two meals each day but complained that food is often not cooked properly; like most prisoners, they told us that they rely on visitors for adequate provisions. A hose at the far end of the cellblock provided the only bathing facility, and it suffers, the boys said, from water shortages and inadequate pressure.[101]

Outside the juvenile cell, prisoners roamed the cell block freely. All the detainees complained about the poor quality of the food, as well as the severe overcrowding, which compels many to sleep on the filthy, roach-infested cell floors. Several interviewees also objected that they had been denied permission to see a doctor. Jefferson, an eighteen-year-old boy, stated that "[p]eople here need to see a doctor, but they don't make them see one because they have no money."[102]

One constable we spoke with said that although a doctor should visit regularly, this rarely happens. Prisoners at Kingston Central, like those detained at Spanish Town, appear to receive medical care only in the case of emergencies, at which time they will be taken to a hospital.[103]

Although only two sixteen-year-olds were held at the time of our visit (the remainder having been transferred the previous day), several adult prisoners confirmed seeing other children held at Kingston Central. One adult prisoner, Clive Dawes, related a particularly disturbing incident that he claimed had occurred on the night preceding our visit. Tajay Brown, a sixteen-year-old, had been severely beaten by the police:

---

[101]Human Rights Watch interviews, Kingston Central Police Station, Kingston, Jamaica, September 3, 1998.

[102]Human Rights Watch interview, Kingston Central Police Station, Kingston, Jamaica, September 3, 1998.

[103]Human Rights Watch interview with constable (name withheld), Kingston Central Police Station, Kingston, Jamaica, September 3, 1998.

[T]hem beat the little man, the juvenile, them beat him and kick
his head, them kick him into gate and step on him throat . . .
.[T]hem carry him gone from [here] last night . . . Inspector
Robbie, him there, but him say nothing.[104]

Thomas, a nineteen-year-old detainee who had been remanded four times during
his two months at Kingston Central, said that he had observed an eleven-year-old
boy who was detained for approximately two weeks.

Halfway Tree

Halfway Tree, a lockup notorious for poor sanitary conditions, was visited
by a Human Rights Watch research team in 1994. The 1994 team found filthy and
overcrowded conditions, and also found that the Halfway Tree lockup was used to
detain numerous children, some as young as ten.[105]

On our visit to Jamaica, however, we were unable to visit the cells or
speak to any detainees at the Halfway Tree lockup. Although Police Commissioner
Forbes had urged us to visit Halfway Tree and had promised to arrange our visit,
we were told upon our arrival at the facility that we would not be permitted to
enter, "since no juveniles [were] held at Halfway Tree." [106]

It seems likely that conditions at Halfway Tree are no better now than they
were in 1994, although our inability to tour the cells makes it impossible for us to
say for certain. Commissioner Forbes himself described the stench emanating from
the Halfway Tree lockups as severe enough to make it difficult for visitors to
breathe. It was of course impossible for us to ascertain whether or not any children
were held at Halfway Tree on the day of our abortive attempt to visit, but several
children we interviewed later, in facilities run by the Department of Children's
Services, told us that they had spent time in the Halfway Tree lockups within the
past two years.

---

[104]Human Rights Watch interview, Kingston Central Police Station, Kingston,
Jamaica, September 3, 1998.

[105]Human Rights Watch, *Jamaica: Children Improperly Detained* (New York:
Human Rights Watch, 1994), pp. 15-16.

[106]Human Rights Watch interview with Deputy Superintendent Lawrence, Halfway
Tree Police Station, Jamaica, September 2, 1998, and telephone interview with
Superintendent Fairclough at police headquarters, Kingston, Jamaica, September 2, 1998.

Gun Court

The Gun Court police lockup in Kingston lies adjacent to the court building in which, as its name suggests, gun-related crimes are tried. Human Rights Watch visited the Gun Court facility on the afternoon of September 2, 1998.

Upon arriving, we were met by Inspector Broomfield, whom we interviewed briefly. Asked about the circumstances of juveniles in the Gun Court, he replied, "[W]e try to treat them well, but some of them don't deserve it."[107] Inspector Broomfield introduced us to Inspector Smith, who oversees the lockup, and he informed us that seventy detainees were currently held at the Gun Court lockup but that we could not enter the cellblock itself "because of the potential for prejudicing those who would be going before an ID parade."[108] The Human Rights Watch team could not privately interview any of the children held at Gun Court, although they met with a number of eighteen and nineteen-year-old detainees in a small office next to the cell block. Although the windows and door remained open and a police constable was stationed outside the open door, limited discussions were possible concerning basic conditions within Gun Court lockup.

Descriptions of conditions within the Gun Court lockup suggest that they substantially resemble the appalling conditions we found at Spanish Town.

• **Ernest**, an eighteen-year-old boy, told us that he had been detained for three months in a five by ten foot cell with four other adults. He complained of the absence of floor space for sleeping and described being kicked in the eye by a guard on one occasion, which, he said, caused a gash over his eye that appeared to be infected.[109]

• **Marlon,** another eighteen-year-old, had been transferred to the Gun Court from Hunt's Bay lockup on March 15, 1998, after a court appearance. He told us that he shared his five by ten foot cell with six other adults. Like Ernest, he complained of the severe overcrowding and of being forced to sleep on the filthy floor. He also stated that staff provide only one meal a day, typically a mixture of rice and chicken, but that "you can't really

---

[107]Human Rights Watch interview with Inspector Broomfield, Gun Court Police Station, Kingston, Jamaica, September 2, 1998.

[108]Human Rights Watch interview with Inspector Smith, Gun Court Police Station, Kingston, Jamaica, September 2, 1998.

[109]Human Rights Watch interview, Gun Court Police Station, Kingston, Jamaica, September 2, 1998.

eat it because it makes you sick."[110] Marlon affirmed that fist fights among the prisoners are not uncommon and that the constables often break up these fights with their batons. He described being beaten by the police on several occasions. One time, he recalled, after being refused permission to leave his cell to use the bathroom, his anger provoked four constables to beat him with their batons, causing him a head injury and nose bleed.[111]

- **John,** a 19-year old, had also been transferred from the Hunt's Bay lockup to the Gun Court Lockup. He told us that he had requested the transfer, because conditions in Hunt's Bay were particularly appalling: the heat and lack of water there made life unbearable. He described his treatment at the Gun Court in similar terms: "[The police] treat us like a dog. When we want to use the bathroom, we have to beg, and sometimes even then they ignore us. Some of the guards have human feelings, but others have none at all."[112] John said that detainees are not permitted to write or receive letters, but that detainees sometimes succeed in smuggling letters in and out during visiting hours.[113]

Inspector Smith's list of detainees listed no detainees under the age of seventeen. Several of our sources suggested, however, that the detention of younger boys at the Gun Court is not uncommon. Since we were not permitted to visit the cells themselves, Human Rights Watch was unable to confirm the presence of children within the Gun Court.

"Juvenile Lockups"

Both Jamaican law and international standards state that detained children must be separated from adult prisoners.[114] According to Police Commissioner Forbes, the Jamaican police have struggled to enforce this policy.[115] Because few,

---

[110]Human Rights Watch interview, Gun Court Police Station, Kingston, Jamaica, September 2, 1998.

[111]Ibid.

[112]Human Rights Watch interview, Gun Court Police Station, Kingston, Jamaica, September 2, 1998.

[113]Ibid.

[114] See Juveniles Act, Art. 17; Beijing Rules, Art. 13.3; U.N. Rules, Art. *See also* Standard Minimum Rules, Art. 30.

[115] Human Rights Watch interview with Francis Forbes, August, 28, 1998.

if any, existing police lockups have appropriate facilities for effectively separating adult and child detainees, the Jamaican police have resorted, in some instances, to utilizing small police sub-stations—with one or two cells—as de facto "juvenile police lockups" where only children are detained.

We visited two "juvenile police lockups," Ewerton and Matilda's Corner. The physical conditions at these lockups—in terms of space, ventilation, sleeping materials, and sanitation—were as bad, and in some ways even worse than the conditions in most of the adult lockups that we visited. Moreover, in neither "juvenile lockup" did the children have the opportunity to exercise or continue their education. Many children in these lockups complained that they were not even regularly fed.

Ewarton Police Station and Juvenile Lockup

At the Spanish Town Police Station in St. Catherine-North Parish, Superintendent Adams explained that children who are picked up by police in this area are usually moved to Ewarton Police Station, some fifteen miles north of Spanish Town.[116] Adams told us that children may be detained at Ewarton for six to twelve months awaiting trial (for those children charged with an offense) or relocation to a place of safety (for those children "in need of care and protection").[117] When the Human Rights Watch team visited Ewarton, we discovered that almost all of the children, including those in need of care and protection, had spent several months in the lockup, in violation of Jamaican law.[118]

Under international standards, children in detention should have access to clean sleeping accommodations and sanitary facilities adequate to their health and privacy needs.[119] During the Human Rights Watch visit to Ewarton, we found seven children, aged thirteen to sixteen years, locked up in two cells with dimensions of approximately eight by five feet. There were no mattresses, cots, or ledges for the children to sleep on. Instead, the children rested on pieces of cardboard and newspaper soaked in water from a leaking shower across the passageway. The floor was sodden, and the children themselves were damp, as there were no dry places to sit or lie down. The shower and toilet were completely open to the two cells, and afforded the children no privacy to bathe or use the toilet.

---

[116] Human Rights Watch interview with Superintendent Adams, August 29, 1998.

[117] Ibid.

[118] Pursuant to the Jamaica Juveniles Act, a court can issue an interim order remanding a child for up to thirty days, but "children in need of care and protection" should not be remanded more than twice.

[119] U.N. Rules, Art. 42.

From our discussion with the children and the police officers at Ewarton, we learned that the children were not permitted to leave the cells for exercise, nor did they have any access to educational materials in the dimly lit cells. Those children whose families had been contacted were able to receive visitors two times per week. According to the U.N. Rules for the Protection of Juveniles Deprived of Their Liberty, children in police custody must be provided with education, preferably at an institution away from the detention facility, medical treatment, and a physical environment with adequate provision for recreation and exercise.[120]

The boys held at Ewarton were charged with various offenses, from serious crimes to petty theft. Some were held because they were in need of care and protection. Although there were two cells, the police at Ewarton made no effort to separate the children according to age or severity of offense.[121] None of the boys knew whether they had an attorney. Two had been detained for only a week, while the others had been detained for several months.

- **Lane,** a very small thirteen-year-old boy, had already spent eight months at Ewarton at the time of our visit. He had been arrested initially for stealing a radio. Before being picked up by the police, he was staying with his grandmother because his father had abandoned him and his mother had emigrated from Jamaica. Lane seemed so depressed that he could barely bring himself to speak; he told us that he did not get enough to eat and that the police "slam doors on you" when he asked them questions. He told us that in his eight months at Ewarton, he had never left his cell except to go to court. When a Human Rights Watch interviewer asked Lane what he would change at Ewarton, if he were in charge, Lane simply shrugged, and, looking down at the soggy newspaper that constituted his blanket, replied, "You can't change anything here." Later, after a pause of nearly a minute, he said, "I wish there was a bathroom. And a dry place to sleep."

- **Godfrey,** aged sixteen, had been in Ewarton for four months when we met him. Godfrey had no lawyer to represent him, but had appeared in court several times since being picked up by the police. A police officer

---

[120] U.N. Rules, Arts. 38-40, 47, 49.

[121] Article 8 of the Standard Minimum Rules provides that "different categories of prisoners shall be kept in separate institutions or parts of institutions taking account of their age, sex, criminal record, the legal reason for their detention and the necessities of their treatment."

explained to us that Godfrey's case was stalled in the Family Court because his accuser never showed up to testify against him. Godfrey told us that he and the other boys would stack up the cardboard and newspaper on the floors to try to keep rats out of their cells, and that at night, they would stuff balled up bits of paper into their ears to try to keep ants and roaches from crawling into their ears as they slept.

- **William**, fifteen, shared Godfrey's cell. William has been in Ewarton for three months at the time of our visit. He complained of an earache, but said like Lane that the guards just slam the cell door in his face when he asks if he can see a doctor. Sergeant Mullins, who escorted the Human Rights Watch team to Ewarton, explained that there were no medical facilities for the boys here.[122]

Matilda's Corner Police Station and Juvenile Lockup

When the Human Rights Watch team visited the police lockup at Half-Way Tree Police Station in Kingston, the senior police officer present, Deputy Superintendent Lawrence, asserted that no juveniles were kept in Half-Way Tree.[123] After thirty minutes of discussion, Deputy Superintendent Lawrence and Deputy Commissioner Fairclough (by telephone) denied us access to Half-Way Tree lockup. Lawrence insisted that all of the children brought to Half-Way Tree were transferred to a nearby police sub-station called Matilda's Corner, which was being used as a "juvenile lockup"—similar to Ewarton police lockup. Lawrence informed us that seven children were currently detained at Matilda's Corner.[124]

The team proceeded to Matilda's Corner where we were informed by Sergeant MacIntosh that all seven of the children detained at Matilda's Corner had been taken to Family Court shortly before our arrival that morning.[125] Although there were no children in the lockup, Sergeant MacIntosh permitted us to inspect the one cell in which he said the seven children had been held until that morning.

The cell was approximately five feet by ten feet with two concrete ledges against the walls. Even with the cell door wide open, the room was dark, with no

---

[122] Human Rights Watch interview with Sergeant Mullins, Ewarton Police Station, Jamaica, August 29, 1998.

[123] Human Rights Watch interview with Deputy Superintendent Lawrence, Half-Way Tree Police Station, Kingston, Jamaica, September 2, 1998.

[124] Ibid.

[125] Human Rights Watch interview with Sergeant MacIntosh, Matilda's Corner Police Station, Jamaica, September 2, 1998.

windows and only dim light coming through some small holes in the concrete walls. The cell smelled of urine and feces and the floor was wet.

We asked to see the toilet facilities and were pointed to a toilet and shower in a separate outhouse near the cell. The outhouse was entirely out of use, and we had to make our way past a row of broken-down motorcycles and bicycles to get to it. The toilet was overflowing with excrement and the shower did not work.

Sergeant MacIntosh told us that because the toilet was broken, the children urinate in the cell and the police put a hose through a crack in the wall to hose down the floor and the children. When asked about the practice of hosing down children in the cell rather than allowing them to leave the cell to use the bathroom, MacIntosh commented: "it's hot in there, they [the children] like being hosed down."[126] MacIntosh also explained that children were not allowed to leave the cell for exercise during the day.[127]

Sergeant MacIntosh told us that the seven children who had been transferred shortly before we arrived ranged in age from twelve to sixteen years old. Four of the boys were detained because their parents could not be located, and a court decided that they were "in need of care and protection." The other three boys had been charged with various offenses.

The policy of moving children in police detention to juvenile lockups suggests that the Jamaican police are concerned with separating at least some children from adults in custody. While this policy seems well-intentioned, in practice, it has had an unfortunate secondary consequence—namely, that children are often detained in lockups characterized by physical conditions as, if not more abhorrent than many adult lockups. This is so because the separate "juvenile lockups" are often located in small, geographically remote police stations, with resources even more meager than the more centrally located "adult lockups." The physical conditions in the juvenile lockups—including space, ventilation, sanitation, and lighting—were worse than anything the team witnessed in adult lockups. Juvenile lockups thus represent an improvement insofar as they shield children from abuse at the hands of adult cellmates. But they have not ameliorated—indeed, they may inadvertently worsen—the egregious sanitary conditions in which children continue to be held.

Evidence About Other Police Lockups

In addition to speaking to some of the children held at the police lockups we visited, we also interviewed many children living in institutions run by the

---

126 Ibid.
127 Ibid.

Jamaican Children's Services Division and by the Correctional Services Department. Many of those children had been held in police lockups before being transferred to these other facilities. Their stories of their time in the lockups confirmed our observations.

- **Garfield,** age thirteen, told us that his mother had turned him over to the police because she felt that he was a discipline problem. The family court judge determined that Garfield was "in need of care and protection." After a stint at the Sovereign Police Station in Kingston, Garfield was transferred to Matilda's Corner. He spent almost two weeks there. He told us that the police only allowed him drinking water once a day, and that he and the other boys in the lockup had to urinate in the corner of the cell. The police, he said, occasionally hosed the cell down—and the boys along with it—by sticking a hose through the small window. During his two week stay at Matilda's Corner, Garfield was only allowed to leave his cell for one trip to the Family Court.

- **Miles,** thirteen, spent one night in the August Town police lockup. He told us that he was alone in the cell, which was windowless and dark, with no toilet or shower. "The cell was filled with urine, and there was no bed, so I didn't sleep, I just stood on a piece of newspaper. I had no food, just a bun. The police were horrible. I'd call to ask them to take me to a toilet and they'd never come."

- **Kevin,** who was sixteen when we interviewed him, told us that he had been picked up by police in October 1997, when he was fifteen, and held at the Hunt's Bay police station, a few miles west of Kingston. He told us that he spent two weeks at Hunt's Bay, where his five-by-eight-foot cell was shared by nine other detainees, most of whom were adults.

- **Derek,** a fifteen-year-old, was detained in the Constant Spring lockup for two weeks. He told us that he was kept in a small cell there with nine other prisoners, all adults. The benches for sleeping were inadequate for the number of people in each cell, so three of the bigger, older men slept on the concrete bunks, while Derek and the others prisoners slept on the concrete floor, using old newspapers for bedding. There was a toilet in the cell, but it did not work, and the cell was constantly filthy.

• **Delroy,** who was seventeen when we met him, told us of the three months he spent at the Hunt's Bay Lockup. He described his cell as "hot, nasty, and dirty." Eight prisoners, some of whom were children, shared a five-by-ten-foot cell. The cell had three concrete bunks. Two prisoners slept on each bunk, and the two others slept on the ground, which was covered with dirty newspaper. At Hunt's Bay, Delroy said, prisoners had no access to working toilets. Consequently, they had to defecate into paper bags and then toss the bags into the passage between the cells. Periodically, guards would let the prisoners into the passage to clean up. "We [would] catch a lot of disease down there," Delroy told us. He said that he became quite ill while detained at Hunt's Bay but that the police would not take him to a doctor.

• **Patrick,** a twelve-year-old who had initially been detained at Matilda's Corner, told us that the police there only gave him bread and tea to eat, so he was always hungry.

• **Richard,** thirteen, spent two weeks in a cell at the Hanover police station. His cellmates were three other boys. "They locked me in a dark cell. They gave us tea and bread, but that was all, and it was not enough, and not fresh. There were no windows, and we stayed in the cell all day. It had no toilet. The police were mostly easy on us because we were young, but if we called out too much they got rough."

• **Steve,** fifteen, spent a month at the Spanish Town lockup. He was in a cell with adults. He told us that the food rations were usually spoiled and that the police beat him up when he complained.

• **David,** thirteen, was left alone when his mother went to jail. The police picked him up because he was begging on the campus of the university in Kingston. He told us that the police were "rough": when he said he did not want to go with them they grabbed him by the throat. He was put in a police lockup for three days "in a room with kids and big men who were scary." He was given soup once a day, but said it was not enough to eat.

• **Michael,** a fifteen-year-old boy whose father was unable to care for him and whose mother had disappeared, was detained at the Point Hill lockup after he was accused of stealing his guardian's money. He stayed at that lockup for two weeks. During that time, he was given food only every two days, used a bucket as a toilet, and slept on the floor of his cell.

- **Charmaine,** a thirteen-year-old girl, was taken from home by the police, along with her younger siblings, ages six and seven. She told us that she did not understand why she and her siblings had been taken from home. They were held for twenty-four hours at a Granville police station, where they slept on a bench in the office and were given no food.

- **Dennis,** sixteen, reported that he spent three months in a cell with adults at the Annatto Bay lockup. "There were ten of us in a small cell. There was only grill ventilation and not much light, just one light bulb out in the passage. We had no bedding, and slept on the concrete. We had bread given to us three times a day. No school, no books. There were four cells, and six police officers to guard them. Sometimes the police would fight with prisoners. I had sinus problems, but they wouldn't let me see a doctor. The worst things were that it was dirty and there was not enough to eat, just bread. The police would take things away from you, too, if you had anything visitors brought you."

The Convention on the Rights of the Child[128] and the United Nations Rules for the Protection of Juveniles Deprived of their Liberty[129] require that any facility used to detain children must conform to certain minimum health standards and assure children adequate health care, "both preventive and remedial."[130] Needless to say, detention of Jamaican children in filthy conditions in police lockups violates the children's rights. Such police lockups also constitute a major public health danger.

During our visits to lockups, almost all of which were in crowded metropolitan areas, we repeatedly found that there were no functional toilets or showers, and the stench in the lockups was overwhelming. Overcrowded cells, particularly when combined with a lack of basic sanitation, are a breeding ground for contagious diseases via both fecal-oral contact and airborne routes. Conditions in police lockups pose a public health risk to the detainees, as well as to the police who guard them, and potentially to the people in surrounding areas.

---

[128]CRC, Articles 3, 24, and 37.

[129] U.N. Rules, Arts. 31 and 34.

[130] Ibid., Art. 49. *See also* Beijing Rules, Art. 13.5.

Just as egregiously, in the midst of such appalling conditions and the clear medical risk they present, children and other detainees told us that they were denied access to medical care. The lack of basic medical care was confirmed by our interviews with guards in the lockups, who told us that prisoners saw doctors only on rare occasions.

Similarly, our interviews suggested that many detainees received inadequate food and drinking water. Indeed, most children who received meals got them once a day and even then, some only received biscuits and tea. Often, the children relied on food taken to them by relatives. This violates the requirement that inmates be provided sufficient food and safe drinking water as set forth in the Standard Minimum Rules for the Treatment of Prisoners.[131]

The children we met were locked in sweltering, poorly ventilated cells all day, generally with little room for moving around freely, given the overcrowded conditions. Yet few children reported being permitted to walk around the passageway of the lockups, let alone go outside for fresh air and exercise. This is in violation of international standards which entitles children in detention facilities to "daily free exercise" and to an environment which allows for physical exercise.[132]

The U.N. Rules explicitly give detained children the right to education and vocational training.[133] But all of the children we met reported receiving no education at all during their time in the lockups, not even a book, even when their detention lasted for months on end. The few children we met who had books—mostly religious tracts and Bibles—told us that the books had been brought by their relatives.

Jamaican children held in police lockups are deprived of their most basic human rights. They are held for long periods—often many months—in overcrowded, filthy cells in life-threatening conditions. They receive inadequate food, and spend twenty-four hours breathing in sweltering, fetid air. Although the children are often being held for petty offenses or because they are neglected or abused and are awaiting proper placement, they are often kept in cells with violent adult offenders, and they are at risk of being preyed upon by both older prisoners and by abusive police guards. They rarely have attorneys to represent them, and they are caught up in a dysfunctional court system that abandons them in lockups simply because the legal process is slow and the system does not know what else to do with them.

---

[131] Standard Minimum Rules, Art. 20. *See also* Beijing Rules, Art. 13.1.

[132] U.N. Rules, Art. 47. *See also* Standard Minimum Rules, Art. 21.

[133] U.N. Rules, Art. 38. *See also* Beijing Rules, Art. 13.5, *and* CRC, Art. 28.

At the suggestion of Police Commissioner Forbes, we visited the Portmore Police Station's new lockup to examine a facility that Forbes sees as modern and humane in a way the older police lockups are not.[134] The Portmore facility was still in the final stages of construction when we visited, and no detainees were present. Nonetheless, it was clear that conditions at the Portmore lockup could represent a vast improvement over those we saw at Spanish Town, Ewarton, the Gun Court, Matilda's Corner, and Kingston Central. Three separate cell blocks—intended to hold, respectively, forty men, fifteen women, and ten children—extended in a T-shaped figure from a centrally located, elevated guard post, constructed to permit security officers simultaneous supervision of the detainees in each corridor. The cells were equipped with sliding doors with tamper-proof locks and slatted windows that provided reasonable ventilation. Each also contained tamper-proof running water and toilet facilities, as well as five concrete bunks, one for each prisoner.

Moreover, three additional separate cells had been designated expressly for (1) sick prisoners who might require quarantine; (2) prisoners who might need to be isolated for violence or disciplinary problems; and (3) prisoners in transit who would be held for a very short period of time (under twenty-four hours). The facility was additionally equipped with glass communication booths, permitting detainees to converse with counsel, relatives, or friends through telephones on either side of the glass. Outside the cells a fenced courtyard provided a secure space for exercise. Superintendent McDonald, who oversees the Portmore facility, informed us that a doctor's office would be constructed on the premises and that a physician would visit at least once each week.[135]

Portmore, at least in terms of the physical plant, represents an improvement. Human Rights Watch could not evaluate its effectiveness in practice, since the lockup was not in use. Nonetheless, some preliminary observations bear emphasis. First, the construction of facilities like Portmore (we were informed that a similar lockup was currently undergoing construction in Montego Bay)[136] represents a step towards greater compliance with international human rights standards for detainees. Portmore potentially offers better ventilation, the capacity to separate different classes of prisoners (though Portmore, too, was not designed

---

[134] Human Rights Watch interview with Commissioner Francis Forbes, August 28, 1998.

[135] Human Rights Watch interview with Superintendent McDonald, Portmore Police Station, Jamaica, August 29, 1998.

[136] Ibid.

to segregate prisoners by status), and an area for exercise and modern sanitary facilities.

Yet at the same time, Superintendent McDonald, who oversees Portmore, remarked that "[t]his lockup was built with prisoners and juveniles in mind,"[137] a statement in some tension with Commissioner Forbes' assurance that the police have ceased to detain children in police lockups. It appears, in short, that new facilities like Portmore, while clearly reflecting an improvement in lockup conditions, are being constructed under the assumption that children *will* continue to be held at police lockups.

Intentional Police Abuse

> *If a kid knows he'll get twenty strops on his buttocks, it's a deterrent. I believe in the scripture: don't spare the rod, or you spoil the child.*
>
> — Neville Webb, Jamaica Union of Correctional Officers[138]

> *"We have overcrowding [in lockups] because we have to keep all these unconvicted prisoners. That's when you get atrocities . . . ."*
>
> — Francis Forbes, Commissioner of Police[139]

During our interviews with children in different parts of the system, the Human Rights Watch team commonly heard stories of low-level abuse[140] and neglect and several accounts of serious physical and sexual abuse by police. Compounding this problem, when incidents of police abuse occur, neither the police nor other agencies responsible for children appear capable of discovering the abuse, treating the abused child, or disciplining the guilty officer.

---

[137] Ibid.

[138] Human Rights Watch interview with Neville Webb, August 28, 1998.

[139] Human Rights Watch interview with Commissioner Francis Forbes, August 28, 1998.

[140] By "low-level abuse," we mean limiting or denying food, water, access to bathroom facilities, and exercise. Low-level abuse also includes verbal abuse and rough physical treatment when children are picked up by police, during their incarceration, and during their transfers to court and other facilities. For greater discussion of low-level abuse and neglect, see section on "Neglect, Rough Treatment, Mental Abuse," below.

Physical and Sexual Abuse

Under the Convention on the Rights of the Child, states party are required to "take all appropriate legislative, administrative, social and educational measures to protect the child from all forms of physical or mental violence, injury or abuse, neglect or negligent treatment, maltreatment or exploitation, including sexual abuse, while in the care of parent(s), legal guardian(s) or any other person who has the care of the child."[141]

Notwithstanding the declared commitments to reform of the leadership of the Jamaican police, the Human Rights Watch team heard of one recent instance of sexual abuse and several incidents of other types of physical abuse.

- **Julia**, fifteen, was interviewed in a temporary home run by the Children's Services Division. She told us that she had left home because her father beat her and cut her with a machete. She stayed briefly with her aunt but was beaten with an electrical cord by her aunt's boyfriend. When she ran away from her aunt's home, Julia was picked up by the police and brought to the local police station as a child "in need of care and protection." Because the cells in the local police lockup were filled with adult men, Julia was forced to sleep on the concrete floor in the passageway between cells. During her second night in the lockup, she said, a police officer came to her and asked her age. When she told him, he asked if she had ever had sex. She said no and said that he tied her down with a belt and forcibly had sex with her and beat her.[142]

Julia's story demonstrates powerfully the danger of detaining children in police lockups[143]—even for "a couple of days." When we interviewed Julia one week after the incident she was experiencing lower abdominal pain and a burning sensation when she urinated. She told us that she had not told anyone about being

---

[141] CRC, Art. 19.

[142] Human Rights Watch interview, Glenhope Place of Safety, Kingston, Jamaica, August 31, 1998. The name of the police lockup has been withheld.

[143] It also demonstrates the potential danger inherent in permitting female detainees to be guarded by male security staff. The Standard Minimum Rules provide that "[w]omen prisoners shall be attended and supervised only by women officers." Art. 53(3). Human Rights Watch does not categorically oppose cross-gender guarding; when employed, however, it must be attended by appropriate safeguards to prevent abuses. For a full statement of Human Rights Watch's position on this issue, see Human Rights Watch, *All Too Familiar: Sexual Abuse of Women in U.S. State Prisons* (New York: Human Rights Watch, 1996).

raped. Nor had she received any medical attention. When asked why she had not told anyone of the rape, Julia expressed fear that the staff would tell the other children at the place of safety and that she would become an outcast. While Julia was reluctant to discuss the rape with staff at Glenhope, she also informed Human Rights Watch that no one had asked her about her stay in police custody.[144]

Although this was the only account we heard of sexual abuse by the Jamaican police, accounts of physical abuse were common. Many of the boys we spoke with during visits to places of safety and the Juvenile Remand Center also reported instances of physical abuse by the police.

- **Warren,** a sixteen-year-old whom we interviewed at the Homestead Place of Safety, recalled abuse by police during his two week stay in Point Hill Police Station.[145] Warren left his parents' home after problems with his father, and went to stay with friends of his parents. After some time there, he was accused of stealing money from the house and brought to the police station. Warren told us that the police beat him with an electrical cord, both in his cell and in the guard room. According to Warren, the police beat him in order to get him to confess to stealing the money.[146]

- **Joseph,** a sixteen-year-old we met at the juvenile remand center, described police abuse during his stay in Hunt's Bay police lockup. Joseph was picked up by the police when he was fifteen for gun possession. He spent two weeks in Hunt's Bay lockup and described being beaten by three or four policemen at a time. He told us that he was beaten so badly that his foot was broken.[147]

---

[144] Under international standards, every facility in which juveniles are detained is required to prepare reports detailing information regarding the child's detention, physical, and mental health as soon as possible after reception. *See* U.N. Rules, Arts. 21-26. However, Superintendent McKeowan at Glenhope Place of Safety explained that her staff is only able to collect rudimentary information upon admission (such as name, date of admission). Julia had been at Glenhope for one week and had never been interviewed about her stay in a police lockup. Julia permitted us to inform the Director of Institutions for the Children's Services Division of her situation. She was subsequently taken to a doctor.

[145] Human Rights Watch interview, Homestead Place of Safety, Stoney Hill, September 1, 1998.

[146] Ibid.

[147] Human Rights Watch interview, St. Andrew's Remand Center, September 3, 1998.

Several other boys also told us about being beaten by the police with batons and sticks during their stays in police lockups.[148]

Neglect, Rough Treatment, Mental Abuse

In addition to these reports of serious sexual and physical abuse, the majority of the children interviewed by Human Rights Watch reported rough treatment in police custody, ranging from neglect to mental abuse. During our visit to the Gun Court Police Station, Inspector Broomfield commented on the treatment of children in custody by police. He said, "We try to treat them well but they don't deserve it."[149] This comment seemed to capture the attitude of many police that we interviewed. The Jamaican police appear to view the children in their custody as criminals first and foremost—and as children only secondarily.

While inadequate resources and poor facilities may partially explain the appalling conditions that children face in police lockups, police attitudes toward juveniles in their custody also provide part of the answer. From our interviews with juveniles and police, it is clear that children in police custody are deprived of adequate water, restricted in their use of the toilet and shower, denied any exercise, and, in some instances, forced to stay in cells with adults. In one instance, referred to briefly above, a Jamaican police officer at Matilda's Corner explained why it was necessary to have children urinate in their cells and hose them down through a hole in the wall rather than taking them outside of the cell to use the toilet. He said: "We can't allow them outside. These children are dangerous and they might escape."[150]

This statement reflects an attitude that seemed to be nearly ubiquitous among lower-ranking police officials: to most of the police, children are assumed guilty—and dangerous—until proven innocent, and they are treated as violent felons regardless of their age and regardless of whether they are held for an offense or for their own protection.

---

[148] Human Rights Watch interview with "Mark," a fifteen-year-old at St. Andrew's Juvenile Remand Center, Stoney Hill, September 3, 1998 (describing being beaten with sticks by police in Constant Spring lockup); Human Rights Watch interview with "James," a sixteen-year-old at St. Andrew's Juvenile Remand Center, Stoney Hill, September 3, 1998 (describing being beaten with batons by police in Montego Bay lockup).

[149] Human Rights Watch interview with Inspector Broomfield, September 2, 1998.

[150] Human Rights Watch interview with Sergeant MacIntosh, Matilda's Corner Police Station, Kingston, Jamaica, September 2, 1998.

In none of the adult lockups that we visited during our stay in Jamaica were adult detainees denied all access to the toilets (although in most lockups access to toilets was unjustifiably limited). Yet at Matilda's Corner, where five of the seven children detained had not even been charged with a criminal offense, the police officer in charge forced the children to urinate in their own cells rather than permitting them to leave the cell and go to the toilet ten feet away. The degree of squalor and humiliation detained children must endure seems calculated to erode their sense of dignity and self-worth, while inevitably proving injurious to their physical and mental health.

Inadequate Responses to Police Abuse

Based upon the Human Rights Watch team's interviews, other Jamaican agencies dealing with children who have spent time in police lockups frequently fail to identify instances of police abuse and are therefore unable to provide an abused child with proper care. None of the places of safety that we visited had a formal intake interview for new children. While the police frequently bring children to places of safety, few of the staff in these homes seem to ask the children about their treatment in police custody. Even when instances of police abuse are uncovered, a child may wait several days before receiving medical attention. The team encountered a similar situation in the Juvenile Remand Center.

When police abuse occurs, institutional responses are inadequate. The Jamaican police have an Office of Professional Responsibility which handles civilian complaints, yet several local human rights observers complained that this was an ineffective mechanism for dealing with police abuse. One source observed that there is a conflict of interest in having a branch of the police investigating other police. When there are investigations into abuses, they are frequently delayed for years and send unclear messages to those police guilty of abuses.

V. CHILDREN IN OTHER
STATE-APPROVED INSTITUTIONS

Children's Services Institutions

The Children's Services Division is a central government agency which operates under the Juveniles Act of 1951. The agency is responsible for children who are in need of care and protection, who have committed an offense, or who are deemed uncontrollable but who have not been abandoned.

The agency's program activities involve admitting children, court proceedings, institutions, foster care, and home supervision. Parents or guardians seeking assistance can meet with a Children's Officer; there is one Children's Officer per parish. For children in need of care and protection, the social worker prepares a report on the child's living situation and presents it to the court. The child may then be given a home supervision order or a "fit-person" order.[151] A home supervision order allows the child to go home under the supervision of a probation officer. A fit-person order places the child in a temporary institution pending the court's decision on more permanent placement.

The Children's Services Division operates institutions that house children temporarily, or, more permanently, on a fit-person order. In law, if not in practice, children are to be temporarily housed in places of safety pending an investigation of their case, or placement in a more permanent facility, foster care, adoption, or home on a trial basis. "It is a fact," however, "that children stay in places of safety for longer periods than envisioned in the law, because of placement problems," said Claudette Hemmings, Deputy Director of Institutions for the Children's Services Division.[152] Children with disabilities and chronic illnesses are most difficult to place.

All the institutions run by the Children's Services Division (children's homes and places of safety) provide education to varying degrees. Children who are housed in places of safety are educated within the facility, which have specially trained teachers. Besides academics, children receive training in one or more crafts and skills: woodwork, agriculture, basketry, craft, home economics, and sewing lessons are offered by various institutions. Children who are housed in the more

---

[151] For an explanation of "fit person" orders, see Section III(2)(B) supra.

[152] Human Rights Watch interview with Winston Bowen, Director of Children's Services Division, and Claudette Hemmings, Deputy Director of Institutions, Children's Services Division, Kingston, Jamaica, August 31, 1998.

permanent children's homes may go to school in the community, and also participate in the aforementioned skills training.

The government provides the money for maintenance of the institutions, and officers in the Children's Services Division carry out regular inspections to ensure that institutions comply with government requirements. There is no medical facility at any of the institutions, and none have resident physicians. However, public health personnel visit regularly to provide immunizations, and physicians in the community sometimes also offer voluntary services. Ordinarily, a sick child must be taken outside the institution for medical care.[153]

Human Rights Watch had the opportunity to visit two places of safety and a children's home. In general these institutions were old, and clearly in need of simple refurbishment. They were reasonably clean, however, and the children appeared well cared for by the staff.

One major problem we noted was the reception or "intake" procedure in all of the institutions we visited. For the most part, facility staff made no effort to determine what had happened to the children in the weeks and months before they arrived at the facilities, and there was no standard screening procedure to ascertain any physical or psychological conditions requiring immediate attention. At all of the facilities we visited, staff told us that they thought very few of the facility's children had spent time in police lockups before their arrival, and seemed surprised to discover, after our interviews with children, how many children had been held by police.

Children in government institutions have often been abandoned, neglected, and sexually, physically, and emotionally abused. These children should be thoroughly interviewed upon their arrival at government institutions. Because of the abusive situations from which most of the children have come, it is essential that these children have an initial medical and psychological screening and promptly receive any needed services.

In 1997, places of safety operated by the Children's Services Division were operating only slightly over capacity.[154] The most common reason the police gave Human Rights Watch for the detention of children in lockups was a lack of space in places of safety, but Children's Services officials rejected this explanation. Although there may be a lack of space in individual facilities especially for girls and babies, redistribution to other institutions, however remote, can alleviate the problem. "[The police] have never called us and not gotten a place for a child," said

---

[153] Ibid.

[154] *See* Planning Institute of Jamaica, *Economic and Social Survey Jamaica 1997*, Ch. 24, "Social Development and Welfare", fig. 24.3.

Mrs. Hemmings of Children's Services. All three facilities we visited were under capacity, and Mrs. Hemmings assured Human Rights Watch that from Children's Services' point of view, it would always be "preferable for a child to sleep on the floor if the facility is full rather than to sleep in a lockup."[155]

Musgrave Children's Home

Musgrave Children's Home, situated in St. Andrew, is a home for girls ages eight to eighteen. The facility has a maximum capacity of fifty and had thirty occupants when Human Rights Watch visited.

The building is a former private residence built in the 1950s and currently owned by the government. The main building is single level with slatted windows, and there is an open yard in front of the building. The building contains a multi-purpose area for dining, classroom activities and counseling, and there is also a small room for sewing. The bedrooms, behind the main building, may be occupied by up to five children. The furniture was very worn, but the bedrooms were clean, with well-made beds.

At the time of our visit, the girls in residence were between the ages of ten and eighteen, with the majority between thirteen and fifteen. All had been deemed "in need of care and protection." The typical day begins with chores at 5 a.m. at the Musgrave Children's Home, followed by breakfast, then school. In the afternoon, the girls complete their chores, have lunch and spend the remainder of the day on crafts and extracurricular activities such as dancing and drama. The children have summer programs when school is on vacation. Many of the children have relatives who visit on Sundays and whom they are allowed to visit during the holidays. The children are disciplined by withdrawal of visiting privileges, deprivation of field trips, exclusion from treats, and additional chores. There are two housemothers who work in shifts, so that a housemother is present twenty-four hours per day.

The cost of maintaining one child in this institution is JA$30,000 per month (approximately US$800). There are plans to improve the institution by refurbishment, and provide an area for skills training.[156] "Since the U.N. Convention [on the Rights of the Child] was ratified, there has been a difference in the government's attention to children," said Mrs. Hemmings.[157] According to facility staff, there has been strong community involvement in the Musgrave home,

---

[155]Human Rights Watch Interview with Claudette Hemmings, August 31, 1998.
[156] Human Rights Watch interview with Superintendent Davidson, Musgrave Children's Home, Jamaica, August 31, 1998.
[157] Human Rights Watch interview with Claudette Hemmings, August 31, 1998.

through church groups, social clubs, the Lay Magistrate's Association, and sports organizations. There are also a Big Sister program and volunteer teachers who assist with remedial work.

Some girls go through a transition program for a year after they leave, through a hostel operated by Women Inc., a program primarily for battered women. "There are more success stories than people could ever imagine," says Mrs. Davidson. She acknowledged, however, that there is no standard policy of tracking what happens to girls after they leave.[158]

The girls we interviewed at the Musgrave Children's Home seemed reasonably happy with the environment and services provided by the home and reported no problems with the staff. For the most part, the relations we observed between children and staff seemed cheerful and informal.

Glenhope Place of Safety

The Glenhope Place of Safety for girls houses girls ages eight to eighteen. At the time Human Rights Watch visited this institution, most of the girls were between fourteen and sixteen. The facility has a maximum capacity of ninety, and the occupancy at the time we visited was seventy-one.

Glenhope houses girls who are either "on remand," awaiting an appearance in family court, or are wards of the state, awaiting long-term placement in a children's home. Most often the girls are victims of abuse or runaways who are in need of care and protection. Very few have been charged with offenses, and those are usually crimes of petty larceny. Staff at Glenhope told us that the children housed there are more frequently brought in directly by police officers rather than by children's services. If the facility has occupancy levels above capacity, staff take the child and then transfer her to another facility.[159] The Head Office of the Children's Services Division is responsible for the transfer of children from places of safety to children's homes.[160]

Medical care at Glenhope is provided through a clinic in the community, and a public health nurse visits every two months to administer immunizations. Almost all the children at Glenhope attend school on the premises. The small school focuses on remedial learning, since most of the girls have had their education seriously disrupted before coming to Glenhope. The girls are also taught

---

[158] Human Rights Watch interview with Superintendent Davidson, August 31, 1998.

[159] Human Rights Watch interview with Mrs. McHugh, Superintendent, Glenhope Place of Safety, Jamaica, August 31, 1998.

[160] Human Rights Watch Interview with Claudette Hemmings, August 31, 1998.

home economics and sewing. Staff told us that problems with discipline are infrequent. Infractions are addressed by withdrawing privileges such as outings and by requiring girls who pose discipline problems to kneel in the staff office for a set time in isolation from the other girls.[161]

There were seven to twelve cots in each of Glenhope's bedrooms, and staff told us that the girls were segregated in bedrooms based on the court order which led to their placement at Glenhope: that is, girls who were awaiting placement with a court-appointed "fit-person" (which might mean, in practice, long-term placement in a children's home) were separated at night from girls on remand.

The residential facilities at the Glenhope Place of Safety were dark, with dilapidated furniture and dingy shower areas. Many of the sinks seemed broken. Most of the windows were cemented over—according to staff, this was necessary to prevent harassment of the girls by neighbourhood boys. Each girl had a locker for personal possessions, but most of the lockers were broken; staff told us they had been vandalized by the girls themselves. On the whole, the girls we spoke to seemed demoralized—more so than at the other Children's Services facilities we visited—but we heard no reports of serious problems.

Glenhope Nursery

The Glenhope Nursery, a bright and cheerful building like a day-care center, houses children up to eight years old, the vast majority of whom are in need of care and protection. The facility has a capacity of forty-five, but it had fifty-four occupants when Human Rights Watch visited. For education and recreation, books and audiovisual aids are available. A playground is also situated on the premises. According to staff, ninety percent of the children at the Glenhope nursery are eventually placed in foster homes, and ten percent return home to their parents.

Homestead Place of Safety

Human Rights Watch visited the Homestead Place of Safety for Boys on September 1, 1998. This is a Children's Services facility for boys ages eight to eighteen, many of whom are in need of care and protection. The maximum capacity is approximately fifty. At the time we visited, forty-five boys were housed there. Well-behaved boys from the juvenile remand center—which is run by the Correctional Services department—are sometimes sent to Homestead to when overcrowding threatens the Remand Center.

---

[161] Human Rights Watch Interview with Superintendent McHugh, August 31, 1998.

Most of the boys at Homestead had been charged with petty offenses or no offense at all. Although there seem to be some exceptions, children who have been charged with serious crimes or who are associated with serious adult offenders are sent to the Remand Center rather than to Homestead. In theory, no child should stay at Homestead for more than ninety days, but staff told us that longer stays are not unusual, given the slowness of the legal and placement processes. Children have court appearances every thirty days, but the frequency of court appearances does not, by most accounts, correspond to rapid case disposition.

Homestead staff told us that they have an informal intake procedure during which the children may relate their past experiences. The parents, if available, also provide information. Only recently, staff told us, have they begun to keep files on all the boys. Staff complained that although each child should, in theory, arrive with a complete file from the police, court system, and Children's Services, the record-keeping processes are so poor and slow that often a particular boy is no longer in residence by the time his file arrives.

There are twenty-three people on the Homestead staff, including teachers, skill trainers, and a housemother. Most of the children attend school on the premises. They participate in academic classes (often remedial in nature), woodwork, agriculture, and physical education. There were many citrus trees, banana trees, and vegetable gardens around the grounds, which are used to provide additional food for the children. The boys build furniture such as bunk beds in the woodwork area, and they are required to do chores such as cleaning and farming duties. During our visit, we saw some children who staff told us were mentally or physically challenged, but staff said that there are no special facilities at Homestead for these children with special needs.[162]

There is no basic medical screening done during the Homestead intake procedure, and the facility insists on a medical certificate during intake only if a child has a visible ailment. There are practical nurses at the facility, however. In cases of medical emergency, the children are taken to a hospital.[163]

A handwritten sign on the bulletin board in the main entrance hall at Homestead told staff to "[d]esist from beating students with improper implement . . . . " When we inquired about this, Superintendent Albert Stamp told us while corporal punishment is permitted at Homestead, he had encountered some problems with staff members who failed to mete out such punishments in the approved fashion. When possible, he said, disciplinary problems are addressed by

---

[162]Human Rights Watch Interview with Albert Stamp, Superintendent, Homestead Place of Safety, Jamaica, September 1, 1998.
    [163]Ibid.

counseling, withdrawal of rewards, or specific additional chores, with corporal punishment as a last resort.[164] "Basically I'm against corporal punishment," Stamp told us, "but there are youngsters who will push a certain behavior . . . . Because you are trying to find out which punishment will work, you say, let me try corporal punishment."[165]

- **Devon,** a fifteen-year-old boy, complained that the staff was abusive and told us that he had been beaten with a wrench.

- **Michael,** another fifteen-year-old, reported being hit with a belt in the palms of his hand, but said that he did not blame the staff member for doing this since he had done something wrong.

For the most part, the children we met at Homestead appeared well cared for and reasonably satisfied with the staff and physical conditions. Homestead is a nonsecure facility, and children are not kept behind fences or locked doors but can walk around more or less as they please.

In general, all of the facilities managed by the Children's Services Division seemed to be adequate. While many of the children seemed unhappy and we heard some reports of rough treatment from staff, we heard no reports of serious abuse. In the physical facilities, while bare-bones, were clean and not overcrowded.

Correctional Institutions

> *"We need to come to a rude awakening that some of these juveniles are hardened."*
> -June Jarrett, Director of Juvenile Institutions

The Department of Correctional Services is the government agency that is responsible for juvenile correctional centers. It is under the jurisdiction of the Ministry of Justice and National Security. Correctional Services runs several facilities housing children ages twelve to seventeen who have been found guilty of more serious offenses and repeat offenders who have been issued a correction order by the court. "Correction orders are a last resort after other avenues have been

---

[164]Article 17.3 of the Beijing Rules provides that "[j]uveniles shall not be subject to corporal punishment."

[165]Human Rights Watch interview with Superintendent Stamp, September 1, 1998.

explored," June Jarrett, an official of the Department of Correctional Services, told us.[166] Although "remands" are not technically the responsibility of Correctional Services, Jarrett said, the department has assumed control of the St. Andrew Juvenile Remand Center.

Correctional Services operates three juvenile correctional facilities (two for boys and one for girls), in addition to the Remand Center, but we were unable to visit those facilities, which operate essentially as long-term reform schools for juvenile offenders. Human Rights Watch was told that the St. Andrew Remand Center, which is for boys only, has a maximum capacity of forty-eight, and staff told us that it always operates at maximum capacity.[167] (There is no remand center for girls, but girls accused of serious offenses are sometimes detained under correction orders at the Maxfield Park Girls' Home, which also functions as a place of safety and a children's home.) In 1997, there were 183 children in all four facilities, 178 of whom were males and 113 of whom were children held under new correction orders.[168]

The remand center and correctional facilities have perennial problems in attracting and retaining qualified staff, according to the Jamaican Union of Correctional Officers. In part, the problem is poor wages; Neville Webb, Vice President of the Union of Correctional Officers, told us that Jamaican correctional officers are the lowest paid in the Caribbean.[169] In 1997, the Department of Correctional Services contracted with private security firms to provide some guard services, in order to allow correctional officers to focus more on rehabilitation.[170] However, the facilities that exist for rehabilitation are inadequate, Webb says, and are not geared toward more serious offenders:

> Youths are exposed to bad models and negative politics predominates. The conditions and treatment in the institutions need to be upgraded, but lack of implementation is a major

---

[166]Human Rights Watch Interview with June Jarrett, Director of Juvenile Institutions in the Department of Correctional Services, September 3, 1998.

[167] Human Rights Watch Interview with Colonel John Prescott, Commissioner of Corrections, Ian Miller, and June Jarrett, September 2, 1998.

[168]Human Rights Watch received conflicting accounts of the facilities' maximum capacity from various sources.

[169]Human Rights Watch Interview with Neville Webb, August 28, 1998.

[170] See Planning Institute of Jamaica, *Economic and Social Survey Jamaica 1997*, Chapter 23, "National Security and Justice", section 23.9.

obstacle. The government believes that what exists for juveniles is sufficient.[171]

St. Andrew Remand Center

The Remand Center takes boys who are being detained pending trial for more serious crimes and those awaiting placement in an approved school. However, Human Rights Watch spoke with several boys at the Remand Center who had been remanded in that facility for minor crimes such as petty larceny.

- **Mark**, a thirteen-year-old boy, was remanded into custody for stealing money from his mother. He was given a correction order and at the time of our interview was awaiting placement at one of the correctional facilities.

- **Paul**, a thirteen-year-old boy, had been remanded for three months—for throwing a stone at a woman—when we interviewed him. Paul had initially entered the juvenile justice system after he ran away from home. He was staying at the Copse Place of Safety but ran away. He was eventually returned there for a second stay, only to run away again. When Human Rights Watch interviewed Paul, he told us that he was afraid of someone at home, so he ran away. Nevertheless, he did not like being away from his mother, so he "hustled" on the street close to home.[172]

- **Andrew**, a fourteen-year-old boy who has received awards at the remand center for good behavior and all-round excellence, had been remanded in custody for three months when we met him, after biting his sister.

- **Philip**, a thirteen-year-old, was sent to the Remand Center by the family court "because he gives his mother trouble," according to a remand center staff member. When we met him, he had been at St. Andrews for five months. He had a severely swollen eye and told us that a bigger boy had beaten him.

On entry into the facility, boys go through an intake procedure, which includes documentation of the offense and the child's past living situation. The

---

[171]Human Rights Watch interview with Neville Webb, August 28, 1998.

[172] Hustling refers to selling goods or services, most often, for example, cleaning windshields of automobiles stopped at traffic lights.

staff psychiatrist evaluates children, if the court requests it. The superintendent, a social worker, and a teacher also assess each child, and may refer him for further psychiatric evaluation. The facility maintains case files for each child.[173] There are three medical orderlies on the staff at the remand center, and children are also taken to nurses and doctors in the community as needed and to the University Hospital of the West Indies on an emergency basis.

Children at the remand center take basic and remedial classes. Although the Remand Center is hardly a substitute for the standard elementary school or high school education, many of the children interviewed by Human Rights Watch told us they were pleased with the educational offerings at St. Andrews, limited though they are, and especially pleased at the opportunity for outdoor games such as soccer. The children receive awards on the basis of academic performance, performance in particular skills, and behavior.

In cases of major discipline problems, punitive measures include isolation, withdrawal of privileges, and the assignment of additional chores. Corporal punishment used to be practiced but was prohibited a year ago.[174] The decision to prohibit corporal punishment was made by the administrative authorities within the Department of Correctional Services: "These are children, and the way you deal with adults, is different than the way you deal with children . . . .We are their parents in many cases," said June Jarrett.[175] The prohibition on corporal punishment has been a source of frustration for some correctional officers, who feel that corporal punishment is a critical deterrent.[176]

Within the Remand Center, children are not separated on the basis of their age or the severity of their offense, and several of the children we spoke with complained of physical and sexual abuse from other boys.

---

[173] Human Rights Watch interview with June Jarrett, September 3, 1998.

[174] Human Rights Watch interview with June Jarrett, Ian Miller, and Colonel Prescott, September 2, 1998.

[175] Human Rights Watch interview with June Jarrett, September 2, 1998.

[176] Human Rights Watch interview with Neville Webb, August 31, 1998.

VI. THE SYSTEM AND HOW IT BREAKS DOWN

It's our policy that convicted persons shouldn't be in the same cells as the unconvicted, that juveniles should not be in the same cells as adults, that women should not be in the same cells as men, and that people charged with major crimes shouldn't be kept with people charged with minor crimes. That's our policy. The problem . . . is systems and structures. Unconvicted prisoners and juveniles should not be the responsibility of the police. It's giving the police a job for which they're not properly equipped.

— Francis Forbes, Commissioner of Police[177]

The law is in place, but the practical realities do not conform with the requirements of the law. This is why the conditions remain poor for juveniles in detention.

—Lloyd Barnett, Jamaican Council for Human Rights.[178]

Structural Shortcomings

Governmental agencies and nongovernmental organizations alike agree that inadequate resources and facilities contribute to the poor conditions Jamaican children face in detention.   Because there is inadequate space for both adult and juveniles in the existing remand centers, Jamaican judges order adults and children remanded to police lockups.

Francis Forbes, the Commissioner of Police, complained that ninety percent of the police lockup population are remand cases and that police are not trained to handle remand prisoners, nor are the lockups designed to cope with large numbers of detainees for long periods.[179]   The police superintendents we interviewed at Spanish Town, Portmore, Gun Court, Half-Way Tree, Matilda's Corner, Ewarton, and Kingston-Central police stations echoed the Commissioner's

---

[177]Human Rights Watch interview with Commissioner Francis Forbes, August 28, 1998.

[178]Human Rights Watch interview with Lloyd Barnett, August 28, 1998.

[179] Human Rights Watch interview with Commissioner Francis Forbes, August, 28, 1998.

complaint. Many acknowledged that children—and adult prisoners, for that matter—were treated poorly, but blamed inadequate resources or poor facilities.

For instance, Superintendent Adams at Spanish Town lockup commented that keeping those awaiting trial in police custody is "a little prejudicial" and told us that he wished that the remand cases could be transferred to proper correctional facilities.[180] The capacity of Spanish Town lockup is fifty prisoners. On the day we visited, Superintendent Adams informed us that there were 138 people being held in the lockup.

While juvenile crime has increased dramatically in recent years in Jamaica, the juvenile justice system has not grown adequately to accommodate the added burden. There is only one juvenile remand center—St. Andrew's Juvenile Remand Center in Stoney Hill—with an official capacity of forty-eight.[181] There is no remand facility for girls. And so far, the government seems to have done little to experiment with noninstitutional alternatives for nonviolent young offenders.

The Department of Children's Services reported that there are fourteen places of safety (ten government operated and four private) around the island.[182] Children's Services told us that the number of spaces available in these places of safety is adequate,[183] yet we met many children in police lockups because, police claim, there is no room for them in the Kingston area places of safety. For those children who have been convicted of an offense, there are three juvenile correctional facilities on the island (two for boys, one for girls) which are always at full capacity.[184]

---

[180] Human Rights Watch interview with Superintendent Adams, August 29, 1998.

[181] Human Rights Watch interview with June Jarrett, September 2, 1998.

[182] Human Rights Watch interview with Winston Bowen, August 31, 1998.

[183] Human Rights Watch interview with Claudette Hemmings, August 31, 1998.

[184] Human Rights Watch interview with June Jarrett, September 2, 1998.

System Failures[185]

> *"While the Jamaican government policy [regarding juvenile justice] is good, in practice the system doesn't work. The Jamaican juvenile justice system suffers from stratified and fragmented systems and procedures."*
>
> -Afshan Kahn, UNICEF Representative[186]

While the Jamaican police, the Department of Children's Services, the Family and Juvenile Courts, and the Department of Correctional Services all bear significant legal responsibilities for children in detention under the Jamaican juvenile justice system, poor coordination and overlapping responsibilities often result in what one former Children's Services employee described as children "falling through the cracks of the system."[187]

The result of these system failures is the chronic overincarceration of children, both juvenile offenders and those in need of care and protection, and severe mistreatment of many children in police custody.

Although police are required to contact the Department of Children's Services after taking a child into custody, in practice they frequently fail to do so. The police may choose to detain a child because they do not have the resources (time, transport, telephone) to identify a place of safety and take the child there. For children charged with violent offenses, police are unlikely to find available space in the single juvenile remand center (capacity forty-eight). Moreover, an officer may find the only open spaces in a place of safety to be on another part of the island. In such cases, the police officer will likely detain the child in a police lockup.

The problems of resource scarcity are further aggravated at rural police stations, and children detained there are even less likely to be transferred to a place of safety. One human rights observer we spoke with commented that the attitude of the child may affect the police officer's decision to detain him in a lockup or transfer him to a place of safety.[188] Another suggested that detention in police

---

[185] For an overview of how the system should operate, see "Agencies With Responsibility for Children," in Section III, "Background," supra, pp. 20-22.

[186] Human Rights Watch interview with Afshan Khan, UNICEF Country Representative, Kingston, Jamaica, September 1, 1998.

[187] Human Rights Watch interview with Claudette Parris, former Superintendent, Glenhope Place of Safety, Kingston, August 31, 1998.

[188] Ibid.

lockups awaiting trial has become a form of punishment itself,[189] in blatant violation of international standards for the treatment of pretrial detainees.

While the Department of Children's Services is also authorized under Jamaican law to transfer children to places of safety,[190] it does not currently have the capacity to regularly monitor police lockups and is therefore unlikely to ameliorate this problem, since it only becomes aware of the presence of children in lockups if it is notified by the police.

When children are detained in police lockups, even for a few days, they are exposed to potential abuse and neglect. By the admission of Commissioner Forbes, however, the police are not trained or equipped to handle long-term remanded prisoners.[191] Nor are the police trained to deal with children.

Moreover, because police do not consistently contact the Department of Children's Services when they take custody of a child, important social services are not provided to the child until after his or her first court date. Because a detained child has no children's officer until Children's Services is involved, his family may not be aware of the child's condition, nor is the child likely to have access to medical facilities if needed.

Perhaps most fundamentally, a child has no advocate while he is detained in police custody. The case of Lane, the thirteen-year-old boy who had been detained for eight months in a Ewarton police lockup on a petty theft charge, provides a graphic example of how children can be lost in the system.

Although a child's first court appearance should result in the determination of the child's status, it is often not so in practice. Because Children's Services is often unaware of a child's presence in police custody until the first court appearance, no Children's Officer is appointed before the first court date. As a result, the judge can render a decision with limited information about the child or remand the child pending further investigation of his family situation. In practice, judges most frequently choose the latter.

It is here that facility shortages are critical. If there are no places available in the juvenile remand center, a child will be remanded by the court to the police lockup. While observing a session of the Kingston Family Court, the Human Rights Watch team encountered just such a problem. A fifteen-year-old was returned to Matilda's Corner police lockup by the judge because there was no space

---

[189] Human Rights Watch interview with Leo Aquiano, September 1, 1998.

[190] Juveniles Act, Art.30.

[191] Human Rights Watch interview with Commissioner Francis Forbes, August 28, 1998.

open in the remand center. As we watched, the judge told the boy, "It's not right that young boys should be locked up. Whatever you have done, we can't just give up on you. It's wrong. But there is nothing I can do—I have to send you back [to the lockup] until your trial."

Even when the child has been remanded to a place of safety by the court, the juvenile justice system breaks down. None of the places of safety visited by Human Rights Watch had an adequate formal intake procedure conforming to international standards.[192] Moreover, few superintendents of places of safety received regular reports from children's officers. One official at a place of safety explained that the turnover of children is frequently so fast that he doesn't receive a report about the child until after the child has left the place of safety.[193]

Without proper information about the child, the staff at the place of safety has little chance of acting in the child's best interest—as the case of the fifteen-year-old girl who told us she was raped by police illustrates. Based upon our visits to four places of safety in the Kingston area,[194] it also appears that children frequently remain in these facilities for longer than the ninety day period that several officials mentioned as the maximum time for which a child should remain detained.

Other elements which contribute to the failures of the criminal justice system are the frequent postponement of trial dates for juvenile offenders and court appearances in which the child's status is not resolved nor his case decided because of procedural delays. While the Human Rights Watch team observed that most children in detention had frequent court appearances, judges commonly postponed the proceedings. As one Children's Services official told us, "Juveniles in state facilities spend too much time in limbo, between court appearances, while the family situation is evaluated, or evidence is gathered. It takes too long for the court to issue a final order, and the child may be forced to stay in a police lockup or another facility for weeks or months."[195]

While observing the proceedings of Kingston Family Court, the Human Rights Watch team witnessed evidence of this. Dwight, a fifteen-year-old boy, appeared before the court on September 4, 1998. The case was postponed because

---

[192] *See* U.N. Rules, Art. 21-26.

[193] Human Rights Watch interview with Superintendent Albert Stamp, September 1, 1998.

[194] The Human Rights Watch team visited Lady Musgrave Girls Home, Glenhope Place of Safety, Glenhope Nursery, and Homestead Place of Safety.

[195] Human Rights Watch interview with Ambassador Marjorie Taylor, August 31, 1998.

the Crown could not present its case; one of the key witnesses for the prosecution was absent. Judges Soares, the presiding judge, noted that the trial had been delayed since May 1997 and complained that "these delays can not be fair and just." Notwithstanding the judge's concern for equity, Dwight was sent back to the police lockup at Matilda's Corner to wait for his next court appearance.

VII. CONCLUSION

Jamaican children in police lockups are truly "nobody's children." Whether they are accused of offenses or have been taken into police custody because they are "in need of care and protection," they languish in filthy, overcrowded cells for weeks and months on end. They eat stale, rotten and inadequate food and sleep on damp concrete or urine-soaked bits of newspaper or cardboard, crammed in with other prisoners who are frequently adults accused of violent crimes. The children are rarely permitted out into the fresh air, and receive no regular exercise, education, or health care. At times, they are physically abused by other prisoners or by the police themselves. Meanwhile, Jamaican state agencies vie with one another to disclaim all responsibility for the children's plight.

It doesn't have to be this way: Substantial improvements could be effected by improving coordination between government agencies to ensure that children are not held in police lockups, by allocating resources to create and maintain institutions capable of responding appropriately to the plight of children in need of care and protection and to those children who come into conflict with the law, and by, at a minimum, ensuring that, until these changes become reality, police lockups are made fit places for human beings to live. Not all of these measures can be realized overnight. But by initiating change and encouraging state agencies to assume proactive responsibility for the plight of children, the Jamaican government could begin to comply with its obligations under international human rights law—and to prevent the needless suffering of so many children.

VIII. APPENDICES

APPENDIX A. U.N. Convention on the Rights of the Child

U.N. Convention on the Rights of the Child, G.A. Res. 44/25, annex, 44 U.N. GAOR Supp. (No. 49), p. 167, U.N. Doc. A/44/49 (1989).

PREAMBLE

The States Parties to the present Convention,

Considering that, in accordance with the principles proclaimed in the Charter of the United Nations, recognition of the inherent dignity and of the equal and inalienable rights of all members of the human family is the foundation of freedom, justice and peace in the world,

Bearing in mind that the peoples of the United Nations have, in the Charter, reaffirmed their faith in fundamental human rights and in the dignity and worth of the human person, and have determined to promote social progress and better standards of life in larger freedom,

Recognizing that the United Nations has, in the Universal Declaration of Human Rights and in the International Covenants on Human Rights, proclaimed and agreed that everyone is entitled to all the rights and freedoms set forth therein, without distinction of any kind, such as race, colour, sex, language, religion, political or other opinion, national or social origin, property, birth or other status,

Recalling that, in the Universal Declaration of Human Rights, the United Nations has proclaimed that childhood is entitled to special care and assistance,

Convinced that the family, as the fundamental group of society and the natural environment for the growth and well-being of all its members and particularly children, should be afforded the necessary protection and assistance so that it can fully assume its responsibilities within the community,

Recognizing that the child, for the full and harmonious development of his or her personality, should grow up in a family environment, in an atmosphere of happiness, love and understanding,

Considering that the child should be fully prepared to live an individual life in society, and brought up in the spirit of the ideals proclaimed in the Charter of the United Nations, and in particular in the spirit of peace, dignity, tolerance, freedom, equality and solidarity,

Bearing in mind that the need to extend particular care to the child has been stated in the Geneva Declaration of the Rights of the Child of 1924 and in the Declaration of the Rights of the Child adopted by the General Assembly on 20 November 1959 and recognized in the Universal Declaration of Human Rights, in the International Covenant on Civil and Political Rights (in particular in articles 23 and 24), in the International Covenant on Economic, Social and Cultural Rights (in particular in article 10) and in the statutes and relevant instruments of specialized agencies and international organizations concerned with the welfare of children, '

Bearing in mind that, as indicated in the Declaration of the Rights of the Child, "the child, by reason of his physical and mental immaturity, needs special safeguards and care, including appropriate legal protection, before as well as after birth",

Recalling the provisions of the Declaration on Social and Legal Principles relating to the Protection and Welfare of Children, with Special Reference to Foster Placement and Adoption Nationally and Internationally; the United Nations Standard Minimum Rules for the Administration of Juvenile Justice (The Beijing Rules); and the Declaration on the Protection of Women and Children in Emergency and Armed Conflict,

Recognizing that, in all countries in the world, there are children living in exceptionally difficult conditions, and that such children need special consideration,

Taking due account of the importance of the traditions and cultural values of each people for the protection and harmonious development of the child,

Recognizing the importance of international co-operation for improving the living conditions of children in every country, in particular in the developing countries,

Have agreed as follows:

PART I

Article 1

For the purposes of the present Convention, a child means every human being below the age of eighteen years unless under the law applicable to the child, majority is attained earlier.

Article 2

1. States Parties shall respect and ensure the rights set forth in the present Convention to each child within their jurisdiction without discrimination of any kind, irrespective of the child's or his or her parent's or legal guardian's race, colour, sex, language, religion, political or other opinion, national, ethnic or social origin, property, disability, birth or other status.

2. States Parties shall take all appropriate measures to ensure that the child is protected against all forms of discrimination or punishment on the basis of the status, activities, expressed opinions, or beliefs of the child's parents, legal guardians, or family members.

Article 3

1. In all actions concerning children, whether undertaken by public or private social welfare institutions, courts of law, administrative authorities or legislative bodies, the best interests of the child shall be a primary consideration.

2. States Parties undertake to ensure the child such protection and care as is necessary for his or her well-being, taking into account the rights and duties of his or her parents, legal guardians, or other individuals legally responsible for him or her, and, to this end, shall take all appropriate legislative and administrative measures.

3. States Parties shall ensure that the institutions, services and facilities responsible for the care or protection of children shall conform with the standards established by competent authorities, particularly in the areas of safety, health, in the number and suitability of their staff, as well as competent supervision.

Article 4

States Parties shall undertake all appropriate legislative, administrative, and other measures for the implementation of the rights recognized in the present Convention. With regard to economic, social and cultural rights, States Parties shall undertake such measures to the maximum extent of their available resources and, where needed, within the framework of international co-operation.

Article 5
States Parties shall respect the responsibilities, rights and duties of parents or, where applicable, the members of the extended family or community as provided for by local custom, legal guardians or other persons legally responsible for the child, to provide, in a manner consistent with the evolving capacities of the child, appropriate direction and guidance in the exercise by the child of the rights recognized in the present Convention.

Article 6
1. States Parties recognize that every child has the inherent right to life.

2. States Parties shall ensure to the maximum extent possible the survival and development of the child.

Article 7
1. The child shall be registered immediately after birth and shall have the right from birth to a name, the right to acquire a nationality and. as far as possible, the right to know and be cared for by his or her parents.

2. States Parties shall ensure the implementation of these rights in accordance with their national law and their obligations under the relevant international instruments in this field, in particular where the child would otherwise be stateless.

Article 8
1. States Parties undertake to respect the right of the child to preserve his or her identity, including nationality, name and family relations as recognized by law without unlawful interference.

2. Where a child is illegally deprived of some or all of the elements of his or her identity, States Parties shall provide appropriate assistance and protection, with a view to re-establishing speedily his or her identity.

Article 9
1. States Parties shall ensure that a child shall not be separated from his or her parents against their will, except when competent authorities subject to judicial review determine, in accordance with applicable law and procedures, that such

separation is necessary for the best interests of the child. Such determination may be necessary in a particular case such as one involving abuse or neglect of the child by the parents, or one where the parents are living separately and a decision must be made as to the child's place of residence.

2. In any proceedings pursuant to paragraph 1 of the present article, all interested parties shall be given an opportunity to participate in the proceedings and make their views known.

3. States Parties shall respect the right of the child who is separated from one or both parents to maintain personal relations and direct contact with both parents on a regular basis, except if it is contrary to the child's best interests.

4. Where such separation results from any action initiated by a State Party, such as the detention, imprisonment, exile, deportation or death (including death arising from any cause while the person is in the custody of the State) of one or both parents or of the child, that State Party shall, upon request, provide the parents, the child or, if appropriate, another member of the family with the essential information concerning the whereabouts of the absent member(s) of the family unless the provision of the information would be detrimental to the well-being of the child. States Parties shall further ensure that the submission of such a request shall of itself entail no adverse consequences for the person(s) concerned.

Article 10

1. In accordance with the obligation of States Parties under article 9, paragraph 1, applications by a child or his or her parents to enter or leave a State Party for the purpose of family reunification shall be dealt with by States Parties in a positive, humane and expeditious manner. States Parties shall further ensure that the submission of such a request shall entail no adverse consequences for the applicants and for the members of their family.

2. A child whose parents reside in different States shall have the right to maintain on a regular basis, save in exceptional circumstances personal relations and direct contacts with both parents. Towards that end and in accordance with the obligation of States Parties under article 9, paragraph 1, States Parties shall respect the right of the child and his or her parents to leave any country, including their own, and to enter their own country. The right to leave any country shall be subject only to such restrictions as are prescribed by law and which are necessary to protect the national security, public order (ordre public), public health or morals or the rights

and freedoms of others and are consistent with the other rights recognized in the present Convention.

Article 11

1. States Parties shall take measures to combat the illicit transfer and non-return of children abroad.

2. To this end, States Parties shall promote the conclusion of bilateral or multilateral agreements or accession to existing agreements.

Article 12

1. States Parties shall assure to the child who is capable of forming his or her own views the right to express those views freely in all matters affecting the child, the views of the child being given due weight in accordance with the age and maturity of the child.

2. For this purpose, the child shall in particular be provided the opportunity to be heard in any judicial and administrative proceedings affecting the child, either directly, or through a representative or an appropriate body, in a manner consistent with the procedural rules of national law.

Article 13

1. The child shall have the right to freedom of expression; this right shall include freedom to seek, receive and impart information and ideas of all kinds, regardless of frontiers, either orally, in writing or in print, in the form of art, or through any other media of the child's choice.

2. The exercise of this right may be subject to certain restrictions, but these shall only be such as are provided by law and are necessary:
(a) For respect of the rights or reputations of others; or
(b) For the protection of national security or of public order (ordre public), or of public health or morals.

Article 14

1. States Parties shall respect the right of the child to freedom of thought, conscience and religion.

2. States Parties shall respect the rights and duties of the parents and, when applicable, legal guardians, to provide direction to the child in the exercise of his or her right in a manner consistent with the evolving capacities of the child.

3. Freedom to manifest one's religion or beliefs may be subject only to such limitations as are prescribed by law and are necessary to protect public safety, order, health or morals, or the fundamental rights and freedoms of others.

Article 15

1. States Parties recognize the rights of the child to freedom of association and to freedom of peaceful assembly.

2. No restrictions may be placed on the exercise of these rights other than those imposed in conformity with the law and which are necessary in a democratic society in the interests of national security or public safety, public order (ordre public), the protection of public health or morals or the protection of the rights and freedoms of others.

Article 16

1. No child shall be subjected to arbitrary or unlawful interference with his or her privacy, family, home or correspondence, nor to unlawful attacks on his or her honour and reputation.

2. The child has the right to the protection of the law against such interference or attacks.

Article 17

States Parties recognize the important function performed by the mass media and shall ensure that the child has access to information and material from a diversity of national and international sources, especially those aimed at the promotion of his or her social, spiritual and moral well-being and physical and mental health. To this end, States Parties shall:

(a) Encourage the mass media to disseminate information and material of social and cultural benefit to the child and in accordance with the spirit of article 29;

(b) Encourage international co-operation in the production, exchange and dissemination of such information and material from a diversity of cultural, national and international sources;

(c) Encourage the production and dissemination of children's books;

(d) Encourage the mass media to have particular regard to the linguistic needs of the child who belongs to a minority group or who is indigenous;

(e) Encourage the development of appropriate guidelines for the protection of the child from information and material injurious to his or her well-being, bearing in mind the provisions of articles 13 and 18.

Article 18

1. States Parties shall use their best efforts to ensure recognition of the principle that both parents have common responsibilities for the upbringing and development of the child. Parents or, as the case may be, legal guardians, have the primary responsibility for the upbringing and development of the child. The best interests of the child will be their basic concern.

2. For the purpose of guaranteeing and promoting the rights set forth in the present Convention, States Parties shall render appropriate assistance to parents and legal guardians in the performance of their child-rearing responsibilities and shall ensure the development of institutions, facilities and services for the care of children.

3. States Parties shall take all appropriate measures to ensure that children of working parents have the right to benefit from child-care services and facilities for which they are eligible.

Article 19

1. States Parties shall take all appropriate legislative, administrative, social and educational measures to protect the child from all forms of physical or mental violence, injury or abuse, neglect or negligent treatment, maltreatment or exploitation, including sexual abuse, while in the care of parent(s), legal guardian(s) or any other person who has the care of the child.

2. Such protective measures should, as appropriate, include effective procedures for the establishment of social programmes to provide necessary support for the child and for those who have the care of the child, as well as for other forms of prevention and for identification, reporting, referral, investigation, treatment and follow-up of instances of child maltreatment described heretofore, and, as appropriate, for judicial involvement.

Article 20

1. A child temporarily or permanently deprived of his or her family environment, or in whose own best interests cannot be allowed to remain in that environment, shall be entitled to special protection and assistance provided by the State.

2. States Parties shall in accordance with their national laws ensure alternative care for such a child.

3. Such care could include, inter alia, foster placement, kafalah of Islamic law, adoption or if necessary placement in suitable institutions for the care of children. When considering solutions, due regard shall be paid to the desirability of continuity in a child's upbringing and to the child's ethnic, religious, cultural and linguistic background.

Article 21

States Parties that recognize and/or permit the system of adoption shall ensure that the best interests of the child shall be the paramount consideration and they shall:
(a) Ensure that the adoption of a child is authorized only by competent authorities who determine, in accordance with applicable law and procedures and on the basis of all pertinent and reliable information, that the adoption is permissible in view of the child's status concerning parents, relatives and legal guardians and that, if required, the persons concerned have given their informed consent to the adoption on the basis of such counseling as may be necessary;
(b) Recognize that inter-country adoption may be considered as an alternative means of child's care, if the child cannot be placed in a foster or an adoptive family or cannot in any suitable manner be cared for in the child's country of origin;
(c) Ensure that the child concerned by inter-country adoption enjoys safeguards and standards equivalent to those existing in the case of national adoption;

(d) Take all appropriate measures to ensure that, in inter-country adoption, the placement does not result in improper financial gain for those involved in it;
(e) Promote, where appropriate, the objectives of the present article by concluding bilateral or multilateral arrangements or agreements, and endeavour, within this framework, to ensure that the placement of the child in another country is carried out by competent authorities or organs.

Article 22

1. States Parties shall take appropriate measures to ensure that a child who is seeking refugee status or who is considered a refugee in accordance with applicable

international or domestic law and procedures shall, whether unaccompanied or accompanied by his or her parents or by any other person, receive appropriate protection and humanitarian assistance in the enjoyment of applicable rights set forth in the present Convention and in other international human rights or humanitarian instruments to which the said States are Parties.

2. For this purpose, States Parties shall provide, as they consider appropriate, co-operation in any efforts by the United Nations and other competent intergovernmental organizations or non-governmental organizations co-operating with the United Nations to protect and assist such a child and to trace the parents or other members of the family of any refugee child in order to obtain information necessary for reunification with his or her family. In cases where no parents or other members of the family can be found, the child shall be accorded the same protection as any other child permanently or temporarily deprived of his or her family environment for any reason , as set forth in the present Convention.

Article 23

1. States Parties recognize that a mentally or physically disabled child should enjoy a full and decent life, in conditions which ensure dignity, promote self-reliance and facilitate the child's active participation in the community.

2. States Parties recognize the right of the disabled child to special care and shall encourage and ensure the extension, subject to available resources, to the eligible child and those responsible for his or her care, of assistance for which application is made and which is appropriate to the child's condition and to the circumstances of the parents or others caring for the child.

3. Recognizing the special needs of a disabled child, assistance extended in accordance with paragraph 2 of the present article shall be provided free of charge, whenever possible, taking into account the financial resources of the parents or others caring for the child, and shall be designed to ensure that the disabled child has effective access to and receives education, training, health care services, rehabilitation services, preparation for employment and recreation opportunities in a manner conducive to the child's achieving the fullest possible social integration and individual development, including his or her cultural and spiritual development

4. States Parties shall promote, in the spirit of international cooperation, the exchange of appropriate information in the field of preventive health care and of medical, psychological and functional treatment of disabled children, including

dissemination of and access to information concerning methods of rehabilitation, education and vocational services, with the aim of enabling States Parties to improve their capabilities and skills and to widen their experience in these areas. In this regard, particular account shall be taken of the needs of developing countries.

Article 24

1. States Parties recognize the right of the child to the enjoyment of the highest attainable standard of health and to facilities for the treatment of illness and rehabilitation of health. States Parties shall strive to ensure that no child is deprived of his or her right of access to such health care services.

2. States Parties shall pursue full implementation of this right and, in particular, shall take appropriate measures:
(a) To diminish infant and child mortality;
(b) To ensure the provision of necessary medical assistance and health care to all children with emphasis on the development of primary health care;
(c) To combat disease and malnutrition, including within the framework of primary health care, through, inter alia, the application of readily available technology and through the provision of adequate nutritious foods and clean drinking-water, taking into consideration the dangers and risks of environmental pollution;
(d) To ensure appropriate pre-natal and post-natal health care for mothers;
(e) To ensure that all segments of society, in particular parents and children, are informed, have access to education and are supported in the use of basic knowledge of child health and nutrition, the advantages of breastfeeding, hygiene and environmental sanitation and the prevention of accidents;
(f) To develop preventive health care, guidance for parents and family planning education and services.

3. States Parties shall take all effective and appropriate measures with a view to abolishing traditional practices prejudicial to the health of children.

4. States Parties undertake to promote and encourage international co-operation with a view to achieving progressively the full realization of the right recognized in the present article. In this regard, particular account shall be taken of the needs of developing countries.

Article 25

States Parties recognize the right of a child who has been placed by the competent authorities for the purposes of care, protection or treatment of his or her physical or mental health, to a periodic review of the treatment provided to the child and all other circumstances relevant to his or her placement.

Article 26

1. States Parties shall recognize for every child the right to benefit from social security, including social insurance, and shall take the necessary measures to achieve the full realization of this right in accordance with their national law.

2. The benefits should, where appropriate, be granted, taking into account the resources and the circumstances of the child and persons having responsibility for the maintenance of the child, as well as any other consideration relevant to an application for benefits made by or on behalf of the child.

Article 27

1. States Parties recognize the right of every child to a standard of living adequate for the child's physical, mental, spiritual, moral and social development.

2. The parent(s) or others responsible for the child have the primary responsibility to secure, within their abilities and financial capacities, the conditions of living necessary for the child's development.

3. States Parties, in accordance with national conditions and within their means, shall take appropriate measures to assist parents and others responsible for the child to implement this right and shall in case of need provide material assistance and support programmes, particularly with regard to nutrition, clothing and housing.

4. States Parties shall take all appropriate measures to secure the recovery of maintenance for the child from the parents or other persons having financial responsibility for the child, both within the State Party and from abroad. In particular, where the person having financial responsibility for the child lives in a State different from that of the child, States Parties shall promote the accession to international agreements or the conclusion of such agreements, as well as the making of other appropriate arrangements.

Article 28

1. States Parties recognize the right of the child to education, and with a view to achieving this right progressively and on the basis of equal opportunity, they shall, in particular:

(a) Make primary education compulsory and available free to all;

(b) Encourage the development of different forms of secondary education, including general and vocational education, make them available and accessible to every child, and take appropriate measures such as the introduction of free education and offering financial assistance in case of need;

(c) Make higher education accessible to all on the basis of capacity by every appropriate means;

(d) Make educational and vocational information and guidance available and accessible to all children;

(e) Take measures to encourage regular attendance at schools and the reduction of drop-out rates.

2. States Parties shall take all appropriate measures to ensure that school discipline is administered in a manner consistent with the child's human dignity and in conformity with the present Convention.

3. States Parties shall promote and encourage international cooperation in matters relating to education, in particular with a view to contributing to the elimination of ignorance and illiteracy throughout the world and facilitating access to scientific and technical knowledge and modern teaching methods. In this regard, particular account shall be taken of the needs of developing countries.

Article 29

1. States Parties agree that the education of the child shall be directed to:

(a) The development of the child's personality, talents and mental and physical abilities to their fullest potential;

(b) The development of respect for human rights and fundamental freedoms, and for the principles enshrined in the Charter of the United Nations;

(c) The development of respect for the child's parents, his or her own cultural identity, language and values, for the national values of the country in which the child is living, the country from which he or she may originate, and for civilizations different from his or her own;

(d) The preparation of the child for responsible life in a free society, in the spirit of understanding, peace, tolerance, equality of sexes, and friendship among all peoples, ethnic, national and religious groups and persons of indigenous origin;

(e) The development of respect for the natural environment.

2. No part of the present article or article 28 shall be construed so as to interfere with the liberty of individuals and bodies to establish and direct educational institutions, subject always to the observance of the principle set forth in paragraph 1 of the present article and to the requirements that the education given in such institutions shall conform to such minimum standards as may be laid down by the State.

Article 30

In those States in which ethnic, religious or linguistic minorities or persons of indigenous origin exist, a child belonging to such a minority or who is indigenous shall not be denied the right, in community with other members of his or her group, to enjoy his or her own culture, to profess and practice his or her own religion, or to use his or her own language.

Article 31

1. States Parties recognize the right of the child to rest and leisure, to engage in play and recreational activities appropriate to the age of the child and to participate freely in cultural life and the arts.

2. States Parties shall respect and promote the right of the child to participate fully in cultural and artistic life and shall encourage the provision of appropriate and equal opportunities for cultural, artistic, recreational and leisure activity.

Article 32

1. States Parties recognize the right of the child to be protected from economic exploitation and from performing any work that is likely to be hazardous or to interfere with the child's education, or to be harmful to the child's health or physical, mental, spiritual, moral or social development.

2. States Parties shall take legislative, administrative, social and educational measures to ensure the implementation of the present article. To this end, and having regard to the relevant provisions of other international instruments, States Parties shall in particular:
(a) Provide for a minimum age or minimum ages for admission to employment;
(b) Provide for appropriate regulation of the hours and conditions of employment;
(c) Provide for appropriate penalties or other sanctions to
ensure the effective enforcement of the present article.

Article 33

States Parties shall take all appropriate measures, including legislative, administrative, social and educational measures, to protect children from the illicit use of narcotic drugs and psychotropic substances as defined in the relevant international treaties, and to prevent the use of children in the illicit production and trafficking of such substances.

Article 34

States Parties undertake to protect the child from all forms of sexual exploitation and sexual abuse. For these purposes, States Parties shall in particular take all appropriate national, bilateral and multilateral measures to prevent:

(a) The inducement or coercion of a child to engage in any unlawful sexual activity;

(b) The exploitative use of children in prostitution or other unlawful sexual practices;

(c) The exploitative use of children in pornographic performances and materials.

Article 35

States Parties shall take all appropriate national, bilateral and multilateral measures to prevent the abduction of, the sale of or traffic in children for any purpose or in any form.

Article 36

States Parties shall protect the child against all other forms of exploitation prejudicial to any aspects of the child's welfare.

Article 37

States Parties shall ensure that:

(a) No child shall be subjected to torture or other cruel, inhuman or degrading treatment or punishment. Neither capital punishment nor life imprisonment without possibility of release shall be imposed for offenses committed by persons below eighteen years of age;

(b) No child shall be deprived of his or her liberty unlawfully or arbitrarily. The arrest, detention or imprisonment of a child shall be in conformity with the law and shall be used only as a measure of last resort and for the shortest appropriate period of time;

(c) Every child deprived of liberty shall be treated with
humanity and respect for the inherent dignity of the human person, and in a manner which takes into account the needs of persons of his or her age. In particular, every

child deprived of liberty shall be separated from adults unless it is considered in the child's best interest not to do so and shall have the right to maintain contact with his or her family through correspondence and visits, save in exceptional circumstances;

(d) Every child deprived of his or her liberty shall have the right to prompt access to legal and other appropriate assistance, as well as the right to challenge the legality of the deprivation of his or her liberty before a court or other competent, independent and impartial authority, and to a prompt decision on any such action.

Article 38

1. States Parties undertake to respect and to ensure respect for rules of international humanitarian law applicable to them in armed conflicts which are relevant to the child.

2. States Parties shall take all feasible measures to ensure that persons who have not attained the age of fifteen years do not take a direct part in hostilities.

3. States Parties shall refrain from recruiting any person who has not attained the age of fifteen years into their armed forces. In recruiting among those persons who have attained the age of fifteen years but who have not attained the age of eighteen years, States Parties shall endeavor to give priority to those who are oldest.

4. In accordance with their obligations under international humanitarian law to protect the civilian population in armed conflicts, States Parties shall take all feasible measures to ensure protection and care of children who are affected by an armed conflict.

Article 39

States Parties shall take all appropriate measures to promote physical and psychological recovery and social reintegration of a child victim of: any form of neglect, exploitation, or abuse; torture or any other form of cruel, inhuman or degrading treatment or punishment; or armed conflicts. Such recovery and reintegration shall take place in an environment which fosters the health, self-respect and dignity of the child.

Article 40

1. States Parties recognize the right of every child alleged as, accused of, or recognized as having infringed the penal law to be treated in a manner consistent with the promotion of the child's sense of dignity and worth, which reinforces the

child's respect for the human rights and fundamental freedoms of others and which takes into account the child's age and the desirability of promoting the child's reintegration and the child's assuming a constructive role in society.

2. To this end, and having regard to the relevant provisions of international instruments, States Parties shall, in particular, ensure that:
(a) No child shall be alleged as, be accused of, or recognized as having infringed the penal law by reason of acts or omissions that were not prohibited by national or international law at the time they were committed;
(b) Every child alleged as or accused of having infringed the penal law has at least the following guarantees:

(I) To be presumed innocent until proven guilty according to law;

(ii) To be informed promptly and directly of the charges against him or her, and, if appropriate, through his or her parents or legal guardians, and to have legal or other appropriate assistance in the preparation and presentation of his or her defense;

(iii) To have the matter determined without delay by a competent, independent and impartial authority or judicial body in a fair hearing according to law, in the presence of legal or other appropriate assistance and, unless it is considered not to be in the best interest of the child, in particular, taking into account his or her age or situation, his or her parents or legal guardians;

(iv) Not to be compelled to give testimony or to confess guilt; to examine or have examined adverse witnesses and to obtain the participation and examination of witnesses on his or her behalf under conditions of equality;

(v) If considered to have infringed the penal law, to have this decision and any measures imposed in consequence thereof reviewed by a higher competent, independent and impartial authority or judicial body according to law;

(vi) To have the free assistance of an interpreter if the child cannot understand or speak the language used;

(vii) To have his or her privacy fully respected at all stages of the proceedings.

3. States Parties shall seek to promote the establishment of laws, procedures, authorities and institutions specifically applicable to children alleged as, accused of, or recognized as having infringed the penal law, and, in particular:
(a) The establishment of a minimum age below which children shall be presumed not to have the capacity to infringe the penal law;

(b) Whenever appropriate and desirable, measures for dealing with such children without resorting to judicial proceedings, providing that human rights and legal safeguards are fully respected.

4. A variety of dispositions, such as care, guidance and supervision orders; counseling; probation; foster care; education and vocational training programmes and other alternatives to institutional care shall be available to ensure that children are dealt with in a manner appropriate to their well-being and proportionate both to their circumstances and the offense.

Article 41
Nothing in the present Convention shall affect any provisions which are more conducive to the realization of the rights of the child and which may be contained in:
(a) The law of a State party; or
(b) International law in force for that State.

PART II

Article 42
States Parties undertake to make the principles and provisions of the Convention widely known, by appropriate and active means, to adults and children alike.

Article 43
1. For the purpose of examining the progress made by States Parties in achieving the realization of the obligations undertaken in the present Convention, there shall be established a Committee on the Rights of the Child, which shall carry out the functions hereinafter provided.

2. The Committee shall consist of ten experts of high moral standing and recognized competence in the field covered by this Convention. The members of the Committee shall be elected by States Parties from among their nationals and shall serve in their personal capacity, consideration being given to equitable geographical distribution, as well as to the principal legal systems.

3. The members of the Committee shall be elected by secret ballot from a list of persons nominated by States Parties. Each State Party may nominate one person from among its own nationals.

4. The initial election to the Committee shall be held no later than six months after the date of the entry into force of the present Convention and thereafter every second year. At least four months before the date of each election, the Secretary-General of the United Nations shall address a letter to States Parties inviting them to submit their nominations within two months. The Secretary-General shall subsequently prepare a list in alphabetical order of all persons thus nominated, indicating States Parties which have nominated them, and shall submit it to the States Parties to the present Convention.

5. The elections shall be held at meetings of States Parties convened by the Secretary-General at United Nations Headquarters. At those meetings, for which two thirds of States Parties shall constitute a quorum, the persons elected to the Committee shall be those who obtain the largest number of votes and an absolute majority of the votes of the representatives of States Parties present and voting.

6. The members of the Committee shall be elected for a term of four years. They shall be eligible for re-election if renominated. The term of five of the members elected at the first election shall expire at the end of two years; immediately after the first election, the names of these five members shall be chosen by lot by the Chairman of the meeting.

7. If a member of the Committee dies or resigns or declares that for any other cause he or she can no longer perform the duties of the Committee, the State Party which nominated the member shall appoint another expert from among its nationals to serve for the remainder of the term, subject to the approval of the Committee.

8. The Committee shall establish its own rules of procedure.

9. The Committee shall elect its officers for a period of two years.

10. The meetings of the Committee shall normally be held at United Nations Headquarters or at any other convenient place as determined by the Committee. The Committee shall normally meet annually. The duration of the meetings of the Committee shall be determined, and reviewed, if necessary, by a meeting of the States Parties to the present Convention, subject to the approval of the General Assembly.

11. The Secretary-General of the United Nations shall provide the necessary staff and facilities for the effective performance of the functions of the Committee under the present Convention.

12. With the approval of the General Assembly, the members of the Committee established under the present Convention shall receive emoluments from United Nations resources on such terms and conditions as the Assembly may decide.

Article 44

1. States Parties undertake to submit to the Committee, through the Secretary-General of the United Nations, reports on the measures they have adopted which give effect to the rights recognized herein and on the progress made on the enjoyment of those rights:
(a) Within two years of the entry into force of the Convention for the State Party concerned;
(b) Thereafter every five years.

2. Reports made under the present article shall indicate factors and difficulties, if any, affecting the degree of fulfilment of the obligations under the present Convention. Reports shall also contain sufficient information to provide the Committee with a comprehensive understanding of the implementation of the Convention in the country concerned.

3. A State Party which has submitted a comprehensive initial report to the Committee need not, in its subsequent reports submitted in accordance with paragraph 1 (b) of the present article, repeat basic information previously provided.

4. The Committee may request from States Parties further information relevant to the implementation of the Convention.

5. The Committee shall submit to the General Assembly, through the Economic and Social Council, every two years, reports on its activities.

6. States Parties shall make their reports widely available to the public in their own countries.

Article 45

In order to foster the effective implementation of the Convention and to encourage international co-operation in the field covered by the Convention:

(a) The specialized agencies, the United Nations Children's Fund, and other United Nations organs shall be entitled to be represented at the consideration of the implementation of such provisions of the present Convention as fall within the scope of their mandate. The Committee may invite the specialized agencies, the United Nations Children's Fund and other competent bodies as it may consider appropriate to provide expert advice on the implementation of the Convention in areas falling within the scope of their respective mandates. The Committee may invite the specialized agencies, the United Nations Children's Fund, and other United Nations organs to submit reports on the implementation of the Convention in areas falling within the scope of their activities;

(b) The Committee shall transmit, as it may consider appropriate, to the specialized agencies, the United Nations Children's Fund and other competent bodies, any reports from States Parties that contain a request, or indicate a need, for technical advice or assistance, along with the Committee's observations and suggestions, if any, on these requests or indications;

(c) The Committee may recommend to the General Assembly to request the Secretary-General to undertake on its behalf studies on specific issues relating to the rights of the child;

(d) The Committee may make suggestions and general recommendations based on information received pursuant to articles 44 and 45 of the present Convention. Such suggestions and general recommendations shall be transmitted to any State Party concerned and reported to the General Assembly, together with comments, if any, from States Parties.

PART III

Article 46
The present Convention shall be open for signature by all States.

Article 47
The present Convention is subject to ratification. Instruments of ratification shall be deposited with the Secretary-General of the United Nations.

Article 48
The present Convention shall remain open for accession by any State. The instruments of accession shall be deposited with the Secretary-General of the United Nations.

Article 49

1. The present Convention shall enter into force on the thirtieth day following the date of deposit with the Secretary-General of the United Nations of the twentieth instrument of ratification or accession.

2. For each State ratifying or acceding to the Convention after the deposit of the twentieth instrument of ratification or accession, the Convention shall enter into force on the thirtieth day after the deposit by such State of its instrument of ratification or accession.

Article 50

1. Any State Party may propose an amendment and file it with the Secretary-General of the United Nations. The Secretary-General shall thereupon communicate the proposed amendment to States Parties, with a request that they indicate whether they favor a conference of States Parties for the purpose of considering and voting upon the proposals. In the event that, within four months from the date of such communication, at least one third of the States Parties favor such a conference, the Secretary-General shall convene the conference under the auspices of the United Nations. Any amendment adopted by a majority of States Parties present and voting at the conference shall be submitted to the General Assembly for approval.

2. An amendment adopted in accordance with paragraph 1 of the present article shall enter into force when it has been approved by the General Assembly of the United Nations and accepted by a two-thirds majority of States Parties.

3. When an amendment enters into force, it shall be binding on those States Parties which have accepted it, other States Parties still being bound by the provisions of the present Convention and any earlier amendments which they have accepted.

Article 51

1. The Secretary-General of the United Nations shall receive and circulate to all States the text of reservations made by States at the time of ratification or accession.

2. A reservation incompatible with the object and purpose of the present Convention shall not be permitted.

3. Reservations may be withdrawn at any time by notification to that effect addressed to the Secretary-General of the United Nations, who shall then inform all States. Such notification shall take effect on the date on which it is received by the Secretary-General

Article 52
A State Party may denounce the present Convention by written notification to the Secretary-General of the United Nations. Denunciation becomes effective one year after the date of receipt of the notification by the Secretary-General.

Article 53
The Secretary-General of the United Nations is designated as the depositary of the present Convention.

Article 54
The original of the present Convention, of which the Arabic, Chinese, English, French, Russian and Spanish texts are equally authentic, shall be deposited with the Secretary-General of the United Nations.

IN WITNESS THEREOF the undersigned plenipotentiaries, being duly authorized thereto by their respective governments, have signed the present Convention.

APPENDIX B. U.N. Rules for the Protection of Juveniles Deprived of Their Liberty

United Nations Rules for the Protection of Juveniles Deprived of their Liberty, G.A. Res. 45/113, annex, 45 U.N. GAOR Supp. (No. 49A), p. 205, U.N. Doc. A/45/49 (1990).

I. FUNDAMENTAL PERSPECTIVES

1. The juvenile justice system should uphold the rights and safety and promote the physical and mental well-being of juveniles. Imprisonment should be used as a last resort.

2. Juveniles should only be deprived of their liberty in accordance with the principles and procedures set forth in these Rules and in the United Nations Standard Minimum Rules for the Administration of Juvenile Justice (The Beijing Rules). Deprivation of the liberty of a juvenile should be a disposition of last resort and for the minimum necessary period and should be limited to exceptional cases. The length of the sanction should be determined by the judicial authority, without precluding the possibility of his or her early release.

3. The Rules are intended to establish minimum standards accepted by the United Nations for the protection of juveniles deprived of their liberty in all forms, consistent with human rights and fundamental freedoms, and with a view to counteracting the detrimental effects of all types of detention and to fostering integration in society.

4. The Rules should be applied impartially, without discrimination of any kind as to race, color, sex, age, language, religion, nationality, political or other opinion, cultural beliefs or practices, property, birth or family status, ethnic or social origin, and disability. The religious and cultural beliefs, practices and moral concepts of the juvenile should be respected.

5. The Rules are designed to serve as convenient standards of reference and to provide encouragement and guidance to professionals involved in the management of the juvenile justice system.

6. The Rules should be made readily available to juvenile justice personnel in their national languages. Juveniles who are not fluent in the language spoken by the personnel of the detention facility should have the right to the services of an

interpreter free of charge whenever necessary, in particular during medical examinations and disciplinary proceedings.

7. Where appropriate, States should incorporate the Rules into their legislation or amend it accordingly and provide effective remedies for their breach, including compensation when injuries are inflicted on juveniles. States should also monitor the application of the Rules.

8. The competent authorities should constantly seek to increase the awareness of the public that the care of detained juveniles and preparation for their return to society is a social service of great importance, and to this end active steps should be taken to foster open contacts between the juveniles and the local community.

9. Nothing in the Rules should be interpreted as precluding the application of the relevant United Nations and human rights instruments and standards, recognized by the international community, that are more conducive to ensuring the rights, care and protection of juveniles, children and all young persons.

10. In the event that the practical application of particular Rules contained in sections II to V, inclusive, presents any conflict with the Rules contained in the present section, compliance with the latter shall be regarded as the predominant requirement.

II. SCOPE AND APPLICATION OF THE RULES

11. For the purposes of the Rules, the following definitions should apply:
(a) A juvenile is every person under the age of 18. The age limit below which it should not be permitted to deprive a child of his or her liberty should be determined by law;
(b) The deprivation of liberty means any form of detention or imprisonment or the placement of a person in a public or private custodial setting, from which this person is not permitted to leave at will, by order of any judicial, administrative or other public authority.

12. The deprivation of liberty should be effected in conditions and circumstances which ensure respect for the human rights of juveniles. Juveniles detained in facilities should be guaranteed the benefit of meaningful activities and programmes which would serve to promote and sustain their health and self-respect, to foster

their sense of responsibility and encourage those attitudes and skills that will assist them in developing their potential as members of society.

13. Juveniles deprived of their liberty shall not for any reason related to their status be denied the civil, economic, political, social or cultural rights to which they are entitled under national or international law, and which are compatible with the deprivation of liberty.

14. The protection of the individual rights of juveniles with special regard to the legality of the execution of the detention measures shall be ensured by the competent authority, while the objectives of social integration should be secured by regular inspections and other means of control carried out, according to international standards, national laws and regulations, by a duly constituted body authorized to visit the juveniles and not belonging to the detention facility.

15. The Rules apply to all types and forms of detention facilities in which juveniles are deprived of their liberty. Sections I, II, IV and V of the Rules apply to all detention facilities and institutional settings in which juveniles are detained, and section III applies specifically to juveniles under arrest or awaiting trial.

16. The Rules shall be implemented in the context of the economic, social and cultural conditions prevailing in each Member State.

III. JUVENILES UNDER ARREST OR AWAITING TRIAL

17. Juveniles who are detained under arrest or awaiting trial ("untried") are presumed innocent and shall be treated as such. Detention before trial shall be avoided to the extent possible and limited to exceptional circumstances. Therefore, all efforts shall be made to apply alternative measures. When preventive detention is nevertheless used, juvenile courts and investigative bodies shall give the highest priority to the most expeditious processing of such cases to ensure the shortest possible duration of detention. Untried detainees should be separated from convicted juveniles.

18. The conditions under which an untried juvenile is detained should be consistent with the rules set out below, with additional specific provisions as are necessary and appropriate, given the requirements of the presumption of innocence, the duration of the detention and the legal status and circumstances of the juvenile. These provisions would include, but not necessarily be restricted to, the following:

(a) Juveniles should have the right of legal counsel and be enabled to apply for free legal aid, where such aid is available, and to communicate regularly with their legal advisers. Privacy and confidentiality shall be ensured for such communications;

(b) Juveniles should be provided, where possible, with opportunities to pursue work, with remuneration, and continue education or training, but should not be required to do so. Work, education or training should not cause the continuation of the detention;

(c) Juveniles should receive and retain materials for their leisure and recreation as are compatible with the interests of the administration of justice.

IV. THE MANAGEMENT OF JUVENILE FACILITIES

A. Records

19. All reports, including legal records, medical records and records of disciplinary proceedings, and all other documents relating to the form, content and details of treatment, should be placed in a confidential individual file, which should be kept up to date, accessible only to authorized persons and classified in such a way as to be easily understood. Where possible, every juvenile should have the right to contest any fact or opinion contained in his or her file so as to permit rectification of inaccurate, unfounded or unfair statements. In order to exercise this right, there should be procedures that allow an appropriate third party to have access to and to consult the file on request. Upon release, the records of juveniles shall be sealed, and, at an appropriate time, expunged.

20. No juvenile should be received in any detention facility without a valid commitment order of a judicial, administrative or other public authority. The details of this order should be immediately entered in the register. No juvenile should be detained in any facility where there is no such register.

B. Admission, registration, movement and transfer

21. In every place where juveniles are detained, a complete and secure record of the following information should be kept concerning each juvenile received:

(a) Information on the identity of the juvenile;

(b) The fact of and reasons for commitment and the authority therefor;

(c) The day and hour of admission, transfer and release;

(d) Details of the notifications to parents and guardians on every admission, transfer or release of the juvenile in their care at the time of commitment;

(e) Details of known physical and mental health problems, including drug and alcohol abuse.

22. The information on admission, place, transfer and release should be provided without delay to the parents and guardians or closest relative of the juvenile concerned.

23. As soon as possible after reception, full reports and relevant information on the personal situation and circumstances of each juvenile should be drawn up and submitted to the administration.

24. On admission, all juveniles shall be given a copy of the rules governing the detention facility and a written description of their rights and obligations in a language they can understand, together with the address of the authorities competent to receive complaints, as well as the address of public or private agencies and organizations which provide legal assistance. For those juveniles who are illiterate or who cannot understand the language in the written form, the information should be conveyed in a manner enabling full comprehension.

25. All juveniles should be helped to understand the regulations governing the internal organization of the facility, the goals and methodology of the care provided, the disciplinary requirements and procedures, other authorized methods of seeking information and of making complaints and all such other matters as are necessary to enable them to understand fully their rights and obligations during detention.

26. The transport of juveniles should be carried out at the expense of the administration in conveyances with adequate ventilation and light, in conditions that should in no way subject them to hardship or indignity. Juveniles should not be transferred from one facility to another arbitrarily.

C. Classification and placement

27. As soon as possible after the moment of admission, each juvenile should be interviewed, and a psychological and social report identifying any factors relevant to the specific type and level of care and programme required by the juvenile should be prepared. This report, together with the report prepared by a medical officer who has examined the juvenile upon admission, should be forwarded to the director for purposes of determining the most appropriate placement for the juvenile within the facility and the specific type and level of care and programme

required and to be pursued. When special rehabilitative treatment is required, and the length of stay in the facility permits, trained personnel of the facility should prepare a written, individualized treatment plan specifying treatment objectives and time-frame and the means, stages and delays with which the objectives should be approached.

28. The detention of juveniles should only take place under conditions that take full account of their particular needs, status and special requirements according to their age, personality, sex and type of offense, as well as mental and physical health, and which ensure their protection from harmful influences and risk situations. The principal criterion for the separation of different categories of juveniles deprived of their liberty should be the provision of the type of care best suited to the particular needs of the individuals concerned and the protection of their physical, mental and moral integrity and well-being.

29. In all detention facilities juveniles should be separated from adults, unless they are members of the same family. Under controlled conditions, juveniles may be brought together with carefully selected adults as part of a special programme that has been shown to be beneficial for the juveniles concerned.

30. Open detention facilities for juveniles should be established. Open detention facilities are those with no or minimal security measures. The population in such detention facilities should be as small as possible. The number of juveniles detained in closed facilities should be small enough to enable individualized treatment. Detention facilities for juveniles should be decentralized and of such size as to facilitate access and contact between the juveniles and their families. Small-scale detention facilities should be established and integrated into the social, economic and cultural environment of the community.

D. Physical environment and accommodation
31. Juveniles deprived of their liberty have the right to facilities and services that meet all the requirements of health and human dignity.

32. The design of detention facilities for juveniles and the physical environment should be in keeping with the rehabilitative aim of residential treatment, with due regard to the need of the juvenile for privacy, sensory stimuli, opportunities for association with peers and participation in sports, physical exercise and leisure-time activities. The design and structure of juvenile detention facilities should be such as to minimize the risk of fire and to ensure safe evacuation from the premises.

There should be an effective alarm system in case of fire, as well as formal and drilled procedures to ensure the safety of the juveniles. Detention facilities should not be located in areas where there are known health or other hazards or risks.

33. Sleeping accommodation should normally consist of small group dormitories or individual bedrooms, while bearing in mind local standards. During sleeping hours there should be regular, unobtrusive supervision of all sleeping areas, including individual rooms and group dormitories, in order to ensure the protection of each juvenile. Every juvenile should, in accordance with local or national standards, be provided with separate and sufficient bedding, which should be clean when issued, kept in good order and changed often enough to ensure cleanliness.

34. Sanitary installations should be so located and of a sufficient standard to enable every juvenile to comply, as required, with their physical needs in privacy and in a clean and decent manner.

35. The possession of personal effects is a basic element of the right to privacy and essential to the psychological well-being of the juvenile. The right of every juvenile to possess personal effects and to have adequate storage facilities for them should be fully recognized and respected. Personal effects that the juvenile does not choose to retain or that are confiscated should be placed in safe custody. An inventory thereof should be signed by the juvenile. Steps should be taken to keep them in good condition. All such articles and money should be returned to the juvenile on release, except in so far as he or she has been authorized to spend money or send such property out of the facility. If a juvenile receives or is found in possession of any medicine, the medical officer should decide what use should be made of it.

36. To the extent possible juveniles should have the right to use their own clothing. Detention facilities should ensure that each juvenile has personal clothing suitable for the climate and adequate to ensure good health, and which should in no manner be degrading or humiliating. Juveniles removed from or leaving a facility for any purpose should be allowed to wear their own clothing.

37. Every detention facility shall ensure that every juvenile receives food that is suitably prepared and presented at normal meal times and of a quality and quantity to satisfy the standards of dietetics, hygiene and health and, as far as possible, religious and cultural requirements. Clean drinking water should be available to every juvenile at any time.

E. Education, vocational training and work

38. Every juvenile of compulsory school age has the right to education suited to his or her needs and abilities and designed to prepare him or her for return to society. Such education should be provided outside the detention facility in community schools wherever possible and, in any case, by qualified teachers through programmes integrated with the education system of the country so that, after release, juveniles may continue their education without difficulty. Special attention should be given by the administration of the detention facilities to the education of juveniles of foreign origin or with particular cultural or ethnic needs. Juveniles who are illiterate or have cognitive or learning difficulties should have the right to special education.

39. Juveniles above compulsory school age who wish to continue their education should be permitted and encouraged to do so, and every effort should be made to provide them with access to appropriate educational programmes.

40. Diplomas or educational certificates awarded to juveniles while in detention should not indicate in any way that the juvenile has been institutionalized.

41. Every detention facility should provide access to a library that is adequately stocked with both instructional and recreational books and periodicals suitable for the juveniles, who should be encouraged and enabled to make full use of it.

42. Every juvenile should have the right to receive vocational training in occupations likely to prepare him or her for future employment.

43. With due regard to proper vocational selection and to the requirements of institutional administration, juveniles should be able to choose the type of work they wish to perform.

44. All protective national and international standards applicable to child labor and young workers should apply to juveniles deprived of their liberty.

45. Wherever possible, juveniles should be provided with the opportunity to perform remunerated labor, if possible within the local community, as a complement to the vocational training provided in order to enhance the possibility of finding suitable employment when they return to their communities. The type of work should be such as to provide appropriate training that will be of benefit to the juveniles following release. The organization and methods of work offered in

detention facilities should resemble as closely as possible those of similar work in the community, so as to prepare juveniles for the conditions of normal occupational life.

46. Every juvenile who performs work should have the right to an equitable remuneration. The interests of the juveniles and of their vocational training should not be subordinated to the purpose of making a profit for the detention facility or a third party. Part of the earnings of a juvenile should normally be set aside to constitute a savings fund to be handed over to the juvenile on release. The juvenile should have the right to use the remainder of those earnings to purchase articles for his or her own use or to indemnify the victim injured by his or her offense or to send it to his or her family or other persons outside the detention facility.

F. Recreation

47. Every juvenile should have the right to a suitable amount of time for daily free exercise, in the open air whenever weather permits, during which time appropriate recreational and physical training should normally be provided. Adequate space, installations and equipment should be provided for these activities. Every juvenile should have additional time for daily leisure activities, part of which should be devoted, if the juvenile so wishes, to arts and crafts skill development. The detention facility should ensure that each juvenile is physically able to participate in the available programmes of physical education. Remedial physical education and therapy should be offered, under medical supervision, to juveniles needing it.

G. Religion

48. Every juvenile should be allowed to satisfy the needs of his or her religious and spiritual life, in particular by attending the services or meetings provided in the detention facility or by conducting his or her own services and having possession of the necessary books or items of religious observance and instruction of his or her denomination. If a detention facility contains a sufficient number of juveniles of a given religion, one or more qualified representatives of that religion should be appointed or approved and allowed to hold regular services and to pay pastoral visits in private to juveniles at their request. Every juvenile should have the right to receive visits from a qualified representative of any religion of his or her choice, as well as the right not to participate in religious services and freely to decline religious education, counseling or indoctrination.

H. Medical care

49. Every juvenile shall receive adequate medical care, both preventive and remedial, including dental, ophthalmological and mental health care, as well as pharmaceutical products and special diets as medically indicated. All such medical care should, where possible, be provided to detained juveniles through the appropriate health facilities and services of the community in which the detention facility is located, in order to prevent stigmatization of the juvenile and promote self-respect and integration into the community.

50. Every juvenile has a right to be examined by a physician immediately upon admission to a detention facility, for the purpose of recording any evidence of prior ill-treatment and identifying any physical or mental condition requiring medical attention.

51. The medical services provided to juveniles should seek to detect and should treat any physical or mental illness, substance abuse or other condition that may hinder the integration of the juvenile into society. Every detention facility for juveniles should have immediate access to adequate medical facilities and equipment appropriate to the number and requirements of its residents and staff trained in preventive health care and the handling of medical emergencies. Every juvenile who is ill, who complains of illness or who demonstrates symptoms of physical or mental difficulties, should be examined promptly by a medical officer.

52. Any medical officer who has reason to believe that the physical or mental health of a juvenile has been or will be injuriously affected by continued detention, a hunger strike or any condition of detention should report this fact immediately to the director of the detention facility in question and to the independent authority responsible for safeguarding the well-being of the juvenile.

53. A juvenile who is suffering from mental illness should be treated in a specialized institution under independent medical management. Steps should be taken, by arrangement with appropriate agencies, to ensure any necessary continuation of mental health care after release.

54. Juvenile detention facilities should adopt specialized drug abuse prevention and rehabilitation programmes administered by qualified personnel. These programmes should be adapted to the age, sex and other requirements of the juveniles concerned, and detoxification facilities and services staffed by trained personnel should be available to drug- or alcohol-dependent juveniles.

55. Medicines should be administered only for necessary treatment on medical grounds and, when possible, after having obtained the informed consent of the juvenile concerned. In particular, they must not be administered with a view to eliciting information or a confession, as a punishment or as a means of restraint. Juveniles shall never be testers in the experimental use of drugs and treatment. The administration of any drug should always be authorized and carried out by qualified medical personnel.

I. Notification of illness, injury and death

56. The family or guardian of a juvenile and any other person designated by the juvenile have the right to be informed of the state of health of the juvenile on request and in the event of any important changes in the health of the juvenile. The director of the detention facility should notify immediately the family or guardian of the juvenile concerned, or other designated person, in case of death, illness requiring transfer of the juvenile to an outside medical facility, or a condition requiring clinical care within the detention facility for more than 48 hours. Notification should also be given to the consular authorities of the State of which a foreign juvenile is a citizen.

57. Upon the death of a juvenile during the period of deprivation of liberty, the nearest relative should have the right to inspect the death certificate, see the body and determine the method of disposal of the body. Upon the death of a juvenile in detention, there should be an independent inquiry into the causes of death, the report of which should be made accessible to the nearest relative. This inquiry should also be made when the death of a juvenile occurs within six months from the date of his or her release from the detention facility and there is reason to believe that the death is related to the period of detention.

58. A juvenile should be informed at the earliest possible time of the death, serious illness or injury of any immediate family member and should be provided with the opportunity to attend the funeral of the deceased or go to the bedside of a critically ill relative.

J. Contacts with the wider community

59. Every means should be provided to ensure that juveniles have adequate communication with the outside world, which is an integral part of the right to fair and humane treatment and is essential to the preparation of juveniles for their return to society. Juveniles should be allowed to communicate with their families, friends and other persons or representatives of reputable outside organizations, to

leave detention facilities for a visit to their home and family and to receive special permission to leave the detention facility for educational, vocational or other important reasons. Should the juvenile be serving a sentence, the time spent outside a detention facility should be counted as part of the period of sentence.

60. Every juvenile should have the right to receive regular and frequent visits, in principle once a week and not less than once a month, in circumstances that respect the need of the juvenile for privacy, contact and unrestricted communication with the family and the defense counsel.

61. Every juvenile should have the right to communicate in writing or by telephone at least twice a week with the person of his or her choice, unless legally restricted, and should be assisted as necessary in order effectively to enjoy this right. Every juvenile should have the right to receive correspondence.

62. Juveniles should have the opportunity to keep themselves informed regularly of the news by reading newspapers, periodicals and other publications, through access to radio and television programmes and motion pictures, and through the visits of the representatives of any lawful club or organization in which the juvenile is interested.

K. Limitations of physical restraint and the use of force

63. Recourse to instruments of restraint and to force for any purpose should be prohibited, except as set forth in rule 64 below.

64. Instruments of restraint and force can only be used in exceptional cases, where all other control methods have been exhausted and failed, and only as explicitly authorized and specified by law and regulation. They should not cause humiliation or degradation, and should be used restrictively and only for the shortest possible period of time. By order of the director of the administration, such instruments might be resorted to in order to prevent the juvenile from inflicting self-injury, injuries to others or serious destruction of property. In such instances, the director should at once consult medical and other relevant personnel and report to the higher administrative authority.

65. The carrying and use of weapons by personnel should be prohibited in any facility where juveniles are detained.

L. Disciplinary procedures

66. Any disciplinary measures and procedures should maintain the interest of safety and an ordered community life and should be consistent with the upholding of the inherent dignity of the juvenile and the fundamental objective of institutional care, namely, instilling a sense of justice, self-respect and respect for the basic rights of every person.

67. All disciplinary measures constituting cruel, inhuman or degrading treatment shall be strictly prohibited, including corporal punishment, placement in a dark cell, closed or solitary confinement or any other punishment that may compromise the physical or mental health of the juvenile concerned. The reduction of diet and the restriction or denial of contact with family members should be prohibited for any purpose. Labor should always be viewed as an educational tool and a means of promoting the self-respect of the juvenile in preparing him or her for return to the community and should not be imposed as a disciplinary sanction. No juvenile should be sanctioned more than once for the same disciplinary infraction. Collective sanctions should be prohibited.

68. Legislation or regulations adopted by the competent administrative authority should establish norms concerning the following, taking full account of the fundamental characteristics, needs and rights of juveniles:
(a) Conduct constituting a disciplinary offense;
(b) Type and duration of disciplinary sanctions that may be inflicted;
(c) The authority competent to impose such sanctions;
(d) The authority competent to consider appeals.

69. A report of misconduct should be presented promptly to the competent authority, which should decide on it without undue delay. The competent authority should conduct a thorough examination of the case.

70. No juvenile should be disciplinarily sanctioned except in strict accordance with the terms of the law and regulations in force. No juvenile should be sanctioned unless he or she has been informed of the alleged infraction in a manner appropriate to the full understanding of the juvenile, and given a proper opportunity of presenting his or her defense, including the right of appeal to a competent impartial authority. Complete records should be kept of all disciplinary proceedings.

71. No juveniles should be responsible for disciplinary functions except in the supervision of specified social, educational or sports activities or in self-government programmes.

M. Inspection and complaints

72. Qualified inspectors or an equivalent duly constituted authority not belonging to the administration of the facility should be empowered to conduct inspections on a regular basis and to undertake unannounced inspections on their own initiative, and should enjoy full guarantees of independence in the exercise of this function. Inspectors should have unrestricted access to all persons employed by or working in any facility where juveniles are or may be deprived of their liberty, to all juveniles and to all records of such facilities.

73. Qualified medical officers attached to the inspecting authority or the public health service should participate in the inspections, evaluating compliance with the rules concerning the physical environment, hygiene, accommodation, food, exercise and medical services, as well as any other aspect or conditions of institutional life that affect the physical and mental health of juveniles. Every juvenile should have the right to talk in confidence to any inspecting officer.

74. After completing the inspection, the inspector should be required to submit a report on the findings. The report should include an evaluation of the compliance of the detention facilities with the present rules and relevant provisions of national law, and recommendations regarding any steps considered necessary to ensure compliance with them. Any facts discovered by an inspector that appear to indicate that a violation of legal provisions concerning the rights of juveniles or the operation of a juvenile detention facility has occurred should be communicated to the competent authorities for investigation and prosecution.

75. Every juvenile should have the opportunity of making requests or complaints to the director of the detention facility and to his or her authorized representative.

76. Every juvenile should have the right to make a request or complaint, without censorship as to substance, to the central administration, the judicial authority or other proper authorities through approved channels, and to be informed of the response without delay.

77. Efforts should be made to establish an independent office (ombudsman) to receive and investigate complaints made by juveniles deprived of their liberty and to assist in the achievement of equitable settlements.

78. Every juvenile should have the right to request assistance from family members, legal counselors, humanitarian groups or others where possible, in order to make a complaint. Illiterate juveniles should be provided with assistance should they need to use the services of public or private agencies and organizations which provide legal counsel or which are competent to receive complaints.

N. Return to the community

79. All juveniles should benefit from arrangements designed to assist them in returning to society, family life, education or employment after release. Procedures, including early release, and special courses should be devised to this end.

80. Competent authorities should provide or ensure services to assist juveniles in re-establishing themselves in society and to lessen prejudice against such juveniles. These services should ensure', to the extent possible, that the juvenile is provided with suitable residence, employment, clothing, and sufficient means to maintain himself or herself upon release in order to facilitate successful reintegration. The representatives of agencies providing such services should be consulted and should have access to juveniles while detained, with a view to assisting them in their return to the community.

V. PERSONNEL

81. Personnel should be qualified and include a sufficient number of specialists such as educators, vocational instructors, counselors, social workers, psychiatrists and psychologists. These and other specialist staff should normally be employed on a permanent basis. This should not preclude part-time or volunteer workers when the level of support and training they can provide is appropriate and beneficial. Detention facilities should make use of all remedial, educational, moral, spiritual, and other resources and forms of assistance that are appropriate and available in the community, according to the individual needs and problems of detained juveniles.

82. The administration should provide for the careful selection and recruitment of every grade and type of personnel, since the proper management of detention

facilities depends on their integrity, humanity, ability and professional capacity to deal with juveniles, as well as personal suitability for the work.

83. To secure the foregoing ends, personnel should be appointed as professional officers with adequate remuneration to attract and retain suitable women and men. The personnel of juvenile detention facilities should be continually encouraged to fulfil their duties and obligations in a humane, committed, professional, fair and efficient manner, to conduct themselves at all times in such a way as to deserve and gain the respect of the juveniles, and to provide juveniles with a positive role model and perspective.

84. The administration should introduce forms of organization and management that facilitate communications between different categories of staff in each detention facility so as to enhance cooperation between the various services engaged in the care of juveniles, as well as between staff and the administration, with a view to ensuring that staff directly in contact with juveniles are able to function in conditions favorable to the efficient fulfilment of their duties.

85. The personnel should receive such training as will enable them to carry out their responsibilities effectively, in particular training in child psychology, child welfare and international standards and norms of human rights and the rights of the child, including the present Rules. The personnel should maintain and improve their knowledge and professional capacity by attending courses of in-service training, to be organized at suitable intervals throughout their career.

86. The director of a facility should be adequately qualified for his or her task, with administrative ability and suitable training and experience, and should carry out his or her duties on a full-time basis.

87. In the performance of their duties, personnel of detention facilities should respect and protect the human dignity and fundamental human rights of all juveniles, in particular, as follows:
(a) No member of the detention facility or institutional personnel may inflict, instigate or tolerate any act of torture or any form of harsh, cruel, inhuman or degrading treatment, punishment, correction or discipline under any pretext or circumstance whatsoever;
(b) All personnel should rigorously oppose and combat any act of corruption, reporting it without delay to the competent authorities;

(c) All personnel should respect the present Rules. Personnel who have reason to believe that a serious violation of the present Rules has occurred or is about to occur should report the matter to their superior authorities or organs vested with reviewing or remedial power;

(d) All personnel should ensure the full protection of the physical and mental health of juveniles, including protection from physical, sexual and emotional abuse and exploitation, and should take immediate action to secure medical attention whenever required;

(e) All personnel should respect the right of the juvenile to privacy, and, in particular, should safeguard all confidential matters concerning juveniles or their families learned as a result of their professional capacity;

(f) All personnel should seek to minimize any differences between life inside and outside the detention facility which tend to lessen due respect for the dignity of juveniles as human beings.

APPENDIX C. U.N. Standard Minimum Rules for the Administration of Juvenile Justice

United Nations Standard Minimum Rules for the Administration of Juvenile Justice ("The Beijing Rules"), G.A. Res. 40/33, annex, 40 U.N. GAOR Supp. (No. 53), p. 207, U.N. Doc. A/40/53 (1985).

PART ONE

GENERAL PRINCIPLES

1. Fundamental perspectives
1.1 Member States shall seek, in conformity with their respective general interests, to further the well-being of the juvenile and her or his family.

1.2 Member States shall endeavor to develop conditions that will ensure for the juvenile a meaningful life in the community, which, during that period in life when she or he is most susceptible to deviant behavior, will foster a process of personal development and education that is as free from crime and delinquency as possible.

1.3 Sufficient attention shall be given to positive measures that involve the full mobilization of all possible resources, including the family, volunteers and other community groups, as well as schools and other community institutions, for the purpose of promoting the well-being of the juvenile, with a view to reducing the need for intervention under the law, and of effectively, fairly and humanely dealing with the juvenile in conflict with the law.

1.4 Juvenile justice shall be conceived as an integral part of the national development process of each country, within a comprehensive framework of social justice for all juveniles, thus, at the same time, contributing to the protection of the young and the maintenance of a peaceful order in society.

1.5 These Rules shall be implemented in the context of economic, social and cultural conditions prevailing in each Member State.

1.6 Juvenile justice services shall be systematically developed and coordinated with a view to improving and sustaining the competence of personnel involved in the services, including their methods, approaches and attitudes.

Commentary

These broad fundamental perspectives refer to comprehensive social policy in general and aim at promoting juvenile welfare to the greatest possible extent, which will minimize the necessity of intervention by the juvenile justice system, and in turn, will reduce the harm that may be caused by any intervention. Such care measures for the young, before the onset of delinquency, are basic policy requisites designed to obviate the need for the application of the Rules.

Rules 1.1 to 1.3 point to the important role that a constructive social policy for juveniles will play, inter alia, in the prevention of juvenile crime and delinquency. Rule 1.4 defines juvenile justice as an integral part of social justice for juveniles, while rule 1.6 refers to the necessity of constantly improving juvenile justice, without falling behind the development of progressive social policy for juveniles in general and bearing in mind the need for consistent improvement of staff services.

Rule 1.5 seeks to take account of existing conditions in Member States which would cause the manner of implementation of particular rules necessarily to be different from the manner adopted in other States.

2. Scope of the Rules and definitions used

2.1 The following Standard Minimum Rules shall be applied to juvenile offenders impartially, without distinction of any kind, for example as to race, color, sex, language, religion, political or other opinions, national or social origin, property, birth or other status.

2.2 For purposes of these Rules, the following definitions shall be applied by Member States in a manner which is compatible with their respective legal systems and concepts:

(a) A juvenile is a child or young person who, under the respective legal systems, may be dealt with for an offense in a manner which is different from an adult;

(b) An offense is any behavior (act or omission) that is punishable by law under the respective legal system

(c) A juvenile offender is a child or young person who is alleged to have committed or who has been found to have committed an offense.

2.3 Efforts shall be made to establish, in each national jurisdiction, a set of laws, rules and provisions specifically applicable to juvenile offenders and institutions

and bodies entrusted with the functions of the administration of juvenile justice and designed:
(a) To meet the varying needs of juvenile offenders, while protecting their basic rights;

(b) To meet the needs of society;
(c) To implement the following rules thoroughly and fairly.

Commentary
The Standard Minimum Rules are deliberately formulated so as to be applicable within different legal systems and, at the same time, to set some minimum standards for the handling of juvenile offenders under any definition of a juvenile and under any system of dealing with juvenile offenders. The Rules are always to be applied impartially and without distinction of any kind.

Rule 2.1 therefore stresses the importance of the Rules always being applied impartially and without distinction of any kind. The rule follows the formulation of principle 2 of the Declaration of the Rights of the Child.

Rule 2.2 defines "juvenile" and "offense" as the components of the notion of the "juvenile offender", who is the main subject of these Standard Minimum Rules (see, however, also rules 3 and 4). It should be noted that age limits will depend on, and are explicitly made dependent on, each respective legal system, thus fully respecting the economic, social, political, cultural and legal systems of Member States. This makes for a wide variety of ages coming under the definition of "juvenile", ranging from 7 years to 18 years or above. Such a variety seems inevitable in view of the different national legal systems and does not diminish the impact of these Standard Minimum Rules.

Rule 2.3 is addressed to the necessity of specific national legislation for the optimal implementation of these Standard Minimum Rules, both legally and practically.

3. Extension of the Rules
3.1 The relevant provisions of the Rules shall be applied not only to juvenile offenders but also to juveniles who may be proceeded against for any specific behavior that would not be punishable if committed by an adult.

3.2 Efforts shall be made to extend the principles embodied in the Rules to all juveniles who are dealt with in welfare and care proceedings.

3.3 Efforts shall also be made to extend the principles embodied in the Rules to young adult offenders.

Commentary

Rule 3 extends the protection afforded by the Standard Minimum Rules for the Administration of Juvenile Justice to cover:

(a) The so-called "status offenses" prescribed in various national legal systems where the range of behavior considered to be an offense is wider for juveniles than it is for adults (for example, truancy, school and family disobedience, public drunkenness, etc.) (rule 3.1);

(b) Juvenile welfare and care proceedings (rule 3.2);

(c) Proceedings dealing with young adult offenders, depending of course on each given age limit (rule 3.3).

The extension of the Rules to cover these three areas seems to be justified. Rule 3.1 provides minimum guarantees in those fields, and rule 3.2 is considered a desirable step in the direction of more fair, equitable and humane justice for all juveniles in conflict with the law.

4. Age of criminal responsibility

4.1 In those legal systems recognizing the concept of the age of criminal responsibility for juveniles, the beginning of that age shall not be fixed at too low an age level, bearing in mind the facts of emotional, mental and intellectual maturity.

Commentary

The minimum age of criminal responsibility differs widely owing to history and culture. The modern approach would be to consider whether a child can live up to the moral and psychological components of criminal responsibility; that is, whether a child, by virtue of her or his individual discernment and understanding, can be held responsible for essentially antisocial be ha vi our. If the age of criminal responsibility is fixed too low or if there is no lower age limit at all, the notion of responsibility would become meaningless. In general, there is a close relationship between the notion of responsibility for delinquent or criminal behavior and other social rights and responsibilities (such as marital status, civil majority, etc.).

Efforts should therefore be made to agree on a reasonable lowest age limit that is applicable internationally.

5. Aims of juvenile justice

5. 1 The juvenile justice system shall emphasize the well-being of the juvenile and shall ensure that any reaction to juvenile offenders shall always be in proportion to the circumstances of both the offenders and the offense.

Commentary

Rule 5 refers to two of the most important objectives of juvenile justice. The first objective is the promotion of the well-being of the juvenile. This is the main focus of those legal systems in which juvenile offenders are dealt with by family courts or administrative authorities, but the well-being of the juvenile should also be emphasized in legal systems that follow the criminal court model, thus contributing to the avoidance of merely punitive sanctions. (See also rule 14.)

The second objective is "the principle of proportionality". This principle is well-known as an instrument for curbing punitive sanctions, mostly expressed in terms of just deserts in relation to the gravity of the offense. The response to young offenders should be based on the consideration not only of the gravity of the offense but also of personal circumstances. The individual circumstances of the offender (for example social status, family situation, the harm caused by the offense or other factors affecting personal circumstances) should influence the proportionality of the reactions (for example by having regard to the offender's endeavor to indemnify the victim or to her or his willingness to turn to wholesome and useful life).

By the same token, reactions aiming to ensure the welfare of the young offender may go beyond necessity and therefore infringe upon the fundamental rights of the young individual, as has been observed in some juvenile justice systems. Here, too, the proportionality of the reaction to the circumstances of both the offender and the offense, including the victim, should be safeguarded.

In essence, rule 5 calls for no less and no more than a fair reaction in any given cases of juvenile delinquency and crime. The issues combined in the rule may help to stimulate development in both regards: new and innovative types of reactions are as desirable as precautions against any undue widening of the net of formal social control over juveniles.

6. Scope of discretion

6.1 In view of the varying special needs of juveniles as well as the variety of measures available, appropriate scope for discretion shall be allowed at all stages of proceedings and at the different levels of juvenile justice administration, including investigation, prosecution, adjudication and the follow-up of dispositions.

6.2 Efforts shall be made, however, to ensure sufficient accountability at all stages and levels in the exercise of any such discretion.

6.3 Those who exercise discretion shall be specially qualified or trained to exercise it judiciously and in accordance with their functions and mandates.

Commentary

Rules 6.1, 6.2 and 6.3 combine several important features of effective, fair and humane juvenile justice administration: the need to permit the exercise of discretionary power at all significant levels of processing so that those who make determinations can take the actions deemed to be most appropriate in each individual case; and the need to provide checks and balances in order to curb any abuses of discretionary power and to safeguard the rights of the young offender. Accountability and professionalism are instruments best apt to curb broad discretion. Thus, professional qualifications and expert training are emphasized here as a valuable means of ensuring the judicious exercise of discretion in matters of juvenile offenders. (See also rules 1.6 and 2.2.) The formulation of specific guidelines on the exercise of discretion and the provision of systems of review, appeal and the like in order to permit scrutiny of decisions and accountability are emphasized in this context. Such mechanisms are not specified here, as they do not easily lend themselves to incorporation into international standard minimum rules, which cannot possibly cover all differences in justice systems.

7. Rights of juveniles

7.1 Basic procedural safeguards such as the presumption of innocence, the right to be notified of the charges, the right to remain silent, the right to counsel, the right to the presence of a parent or guardian, the right to confront and cross-examine witnesses and the right to appeal to a higher authority shall be guaranteed at all stages of proceedings.

Commentary

Rule 7.1 emphasizes some important points that represent essential elements for a fair and just trial and that are internationally recognized in existing human rights instruments. (See also rule 14.) The presumption of innocence, for instance, is also to be found in article 11 of the Universal Declaration of Human rights and in article 14, paragraph 2, of the International Covenant on Civil and Political Rights. Rules

14 seq. of these Standard Minimum Rules specify issues that are important for proceedings in juvenile cases, in particular, while rule 7.1 affirms the most basic procedural safeguards in a general way.

8. Protection of privacy
8.1 The juvenile's right to privacy shall be respected at all stages in order to avoid harm being caused to her or him by undue publicity or by the process of labeling.

8.2 In principle, no information that may lead to the identification of a juvenile offender shall be published.

Commentary
Rule 8 stresses the importance of the protection of the juvenile's right to privacy. Young persons are particularly susceptible to stigmatization. Criminological research into labeling processes has provided evidence of the detrimental effects (of different kinds) resulting from the permanent identification of young persons as "delinquent" or "criminal".

Rule 8 stresses the importance of protecting the juvenile from the adverse effects that may result from the publication in the mass media of information about the case (for example the names of young offenders, alleged or convicted). The interest of the individual should be protected and upheld, at least in principle. (The general contents of rule 8 are further specified in rule 2 1.)

9. Saving clause
9.1 Nothing in these Rules shall be interpreted as precluding the application of the Standard Minimum Rules for the Treatment of Prisoners adopted by the United Nations and other human rights instruments and standards recognized by the international community that relate to the care and protection of the young.

Commentary
Rule 9 is meant to avoid any misunderstanding in interpreting and implementing the present Rules in conformity with principles contained in relevant existing or emerging international human rights instruments and standards-such as the Universal Declaration of Human Rights, the International Covenant on Economic, Social and Cultural Rights and the International Covenant on Civil and Political Rights, and the Declaration of the Rights of the Child and the draft convention on the rights of the child. It should be understood that the application of the present

Rules is without prejudice to any such international instruments which may contain provisions of wider application. (See also rule 27.)

PART TWO

INVESTIGATION AND PROSECUTION

10. Initial contact

10.1 Upon the apprehension of a juvenile, her or his parents or guardian shall be immediately notified of such apprehension, and, where such immediate notification is not possible, the parents or guardian shall be notified within the shortest possible time thereafter.

10.2 A judge or other competent official or body shall, without delay, consider the issue of release.

10.3 Contacts between the law enforcement agencies and a juvenile offender shall be managed in such a way as to respect the legal status of the juvenile, promote the well-being of the juvenile and avoid harm to her or him, with due regard to the circumstances of the case.

Commentary

Rule 10.1 is in principle contained in rule 92 of the Standard Minimum Rules for the Treatment of Prisoners.

The question of release (rule 10.2) shall be considered without delay by a judge or other competent official. The latter refers to any person or institution in the broadest sense of the term, including community boards or police authorities having power to release an arrested person. (See also the International Covenant on Civil and Political Rights, article 9, paragraph 3.)

Rule 10.3 deals with some fundamental aspects of the procedures and behavior on the part of the police and other law enforcement officials in cases of juvenile crime. To "avoid harm" admittedly is flexible wording and covers many features of possible interaction (for example the use of harsh language, physical violence or exposure to the environment). Involvement in juvenile justice processes in itself can be "harmful" to juveniles; the term "avoid harm" should be broadly interpreted, therefore, as doing the least harm possible to the juvenile in the first instance, as well as any additional or undue harm. This is especially important in the initial contact with law enforcement agencies, which might profoundly influence the juvenile's attitude towards the State and society. Moreover, the success of any further intervention is largely dependent on such initial contacts. Compassion and kind firmness are important in these situations.

11. Diversion
11.1 Consideration shall be given, wherever appropriate, to dealing with juvenile offenders without resorting to formal trial by the competent authority, referred to in rule 14.1 below.

11.2 The police, the prosecution or other agencies dealing with juvenile cases shall be empowered to dispose of such cases, at their discretion, without recourse to formal hearings, in accordance with the criteria laid down for that purpose in the respective legal system and also in accordance with the principles contained in these Rules.

11.3 Any diversion involving referral to appropriate community or other services shall require the consent of the juvenile, or her or his parents or guardian, provided that such decision to refer a case shall be subject to review by a competent authority, upon application.

11.4 In order to facilitate the discretionary disposition of juvenile cases, efforts shall be made to provide for community programmes, such as temporary supervision and guidance, restitution, and compensation of victims.

Commentary
Diversion, involving removal from criminal justice processing and, frequently, redirection to community support services, is commonly practiced on a formal and informal basis in many legal systems. This practice serves to hinder the negative effects of subsequent proceedings in juvenile justice administration (for example the stigma of conviction and sentence). In many cases, non-intervention would be the best response. Thus, diversion at the outset and without referral to alternative (social) services may be the optimal response. This is especially the case where the offense is of a non-serious nature and where the family, the school or other informal social control institutions have already reacted, or are likely to react, in an appropriate and constructive manner.

As stated in rule 11.2, diversion may be used at any point of decision-making-by the police, the prosecution or other agencies such as the courts, tribunals, boards or councils. It may be exercised by one authority or several or all authorities, according to the rules and policies of the respective systems and in line with the present Rules. It need not necessarily be limited to petty cases, thus rendering diversion an important instrument.

Rule 11.3 stresses the important requirement of securing the consent of the young offender (or the parent or guardian) to the recommended diversionary measure(s). (Diversion to community service without such consent would contradict the Abolition of Forced Labor Convention.) However, this consent should not be left unchallengeable, since it might sometimes be given out of sheer desperation on the part of the juvenile. The rule underlines that care should be taken to minimize the potential for coercion and intimidation at all levels in the diversion process. Juveniles should not feel pressured (for example in order to avoid court appearance) or be pressured into consenting to diversion programmes. Thus, it is advocated that provision should be made for an objective appraisal of the appropriateness of dispositions involving young offenders by a "competent authority upon application". (The "competent authority,' may be different from that referred to in rule 14.)

Rule 11.4 recommends the provision of viable alternatives to juvenile justice processing in the form of community-based diversion. Programmes that involve settlement by victim restitution and those that seek to avoid future conflict with the law through temporary supervision and guidance are especially commended. The merits of individual cases would make diversion appropriate, even when more serious offenses have been committed (for example first offense, the act having been committed under peer pressure, etc.).

12. Specialization within the police
12.1 In order to best fulfil their functions, police officers who frequently or exclusively deal with juveniles or who are primarily engaged in the prevention of juvenile crime shall be specially instructed and trained. In large cities, special police units should be established for that purpose.

Commentary
Rule 12 draws attention to the need for specialized training for all law enforcement officials who are involved in the administration of juvenile justice. As police are the first point of contact with the juvenile justice system, it is most important that they act in an informed and appropriate manner.

While the relationship between urbanization and crime is clearly complex, an increase in juvenile crime has been associated with the growth of large cities, particularly with rapid and unplanned growth. Specialized police units would therefore be indispensable, not only in the interest of implementing specific principles contained in the present instrument (such as rule 1.6) but more generally for improving the prevention and control of juvenile crime and the handling of juvenile offenders.

13. Detention pending trial
13.1 Detention pending trial shall be used only as a measure of last resort and for the shortest possible period of time.

13.2 Whenever possible, detention pending trial shall be replaced by alternative measures, such as close supervision, intensive care or placement with a family or in an educational setting or home.

13.3 Juveniles under detention pending trial shall be entitled to all rights and guarantees of the Standard Minimum Rules for the Treatment of Prisoners adopted by the United Nations.

13.4 Juveniles under detention pending trial shall be kept separate from adults and shall be detained in a separate institution or in a separate part of an institution also holding adults.

13.5 While in custody, juveniles shall receive care, protection and all necessary individual assistance-social, educational, vocational, psychological, medical and physical-that they may require in view of their age, sex and personality.

Commentary
The danger to juveniles of "criminal contamination" while in detention pending trial must not be underestimated. It is therefore important to stress the need for alternative measures. By doing so, rule 13.1 encourages the devising of new and innovative measures to avoid such detention in the interest of the well-being of the juvenile. Juveniles under detention pending trial are entitled to all the rights and guarantees of the Standard Minimum Rules for the Treatment of Prisoners as well as the International Covenant on Civil and Political Rights, especially article 9 and article 10, paragraphs 2 (b) and 3.

Rule 13.4 does not prevent States from taking other measures against the negative influences of adult offenders which are at least as effective as the measures mentioned in the rule.

Different forms of assistance that may become necessary have been enumerated to draw attention to the broad range of particular needs of young detainees to be addressed (for example females or males, drug addicts, alcoholics, mentally ill juveniles, young persons suffering from the trauma, for example, of arrest, etc.).

Varying physical and psychological characteristics of young detainees may warrant classification measures by which some are kept separate while in detention pending trial, thus contributing to the avoidance of victimization and rendering more appropriate assistance.

The Sixth United Nations Congress on the Prevention of Crime and the Treatment of Offenders, in its resolution 4 on juvenile justice standards, specified that the Rules, inter alia, should reflect the basic principle that pre-trial detention should be used only as a last resort, that no minors should be held in a facility where they are vulnerable to the negative influences of adult detainees and that account should always be taken of the needs particular to their stage of development.

PART THREE

ADJUDICATION AND DISPOSITION

14. Competent authority to adjudicate
14.1 Where the case of a juvenile offender has not been diverted (under rule 11), she or he shall be dealt with by the competent authority (court, tribunal, board, council, etc.) according to the principles of a fair and just trial.

14.2 The proceedings shall be conducive to the best interests of the juvenile and shall be conducted in an atmosphere of understanding, which shall allow the juvenile to participate therein and to express herself or himself freely.

Commentary
It is difficult to formulate a definition of the competent body or person that would universally describe an adjudicating authority. "Competent authority" is meant to include those who preside over courts or tribunals (composed of a single judge or of several members), including professional and lay magistrates as well as

administrative boards (for example the Scottish and Scandinavian systems) or other more informal community and conflict resolution agencies of an adjudicatory nature. The procedure for dealing with juvenile offenders shall in any case follow the minimum standards that are applied almost universally for any criminal defendant under the procedure known as "due process of law". In accordance with due process, a "fair and just trial" includes such basic safeguards as the presumption of innocence, the presentation and examination of witnesses, the common legal defenses, the right to remain silent, the right to have the last word in a hearing, the right to appeal, etc. (See also rule 7.1.)

15. Legal counsel, parents and guardians

15.1 Throughout the proceedings the juvenile shall have the right to be represented by a legal adviser or to apply for free legal aid where there is provision for such aid in the country.

15.2 The parents or the guardian shall be entitled to participate in the proceedings and may be required by the competent authority to attend them in the interest of the juvenile. They may, however, be denied participation by the competent authority if there are reasons to assume that such exclusion is necessary in the interest of the juvenile.

Commentary

Rule 15.1 uses terminology similar to that found in rule 93 of the Standard Minimum Rules for the Treatment of Prisoners. Whereas legal counsel and free legal aid are needed to assure the juvenile legal assistance, the right of the parents or guardian to participate as stated in rule 15.2 should be viewed as general psychological and emotional assistance to the juvenile-a function extending throughout the procedure.

The competent authority's search for an adequate disposition of the case may pro fit, in particular, fro m the co-operation of the legal representatives of the juvenile (or, for that matter, some other personal assistant who the juvenile can and does really trust). Such concern can be thwarted if the presence of parents or guardians at the hearings plays a negative role, for instance, if they display a hostile attitude towards the juvenile, hence, the possibility of their exclusion must be provided for.

16. Social inquiry reports

16.1 In all cases except those involving minor offenses, before the competent authority renders a final disposition prior to sentencing, the background and circumstances in which the juvenile is living or the conditions under which the offense has been committed shall be properly investigated so as to facilitate judicious adjudication of the case by the competent authority.

Commentary
Social inquiry reports (social reports or pre-sentence reports) are an indispensable aid in most legal proceedings involving juveniles. The competent authority should be informed of relevant facts about the juvenile, such as social an d family background, school career, educational experiences, etc. For this purpose, some jurisdictions use special social services or personnel attached to the court or board. Other personnel, including probation officers, may serve the same function. The rule therefore requires that adequate social services should be available to deliver social inquiry reports of a qualified nature.

17. Guiding principles in adjudication and disposition
17.1 The disposition of the competent authority shall be guided by the following principles:
(a) The reaction taken shall always be in proportion not only to the circumstances and the gravity of the offense but also to the circumstances and the needs of the juvenile as well as to the needs of the society;
(b) Restrictions on the personal liberty of the juvenile shall be imposed only after careful consideration and shall be limited to the possible minimum;
(c) Deprivation of personal liberty shall not be imposed unless the juvenile is adjudicated of a serious act involving violence against another person or of persistence in committing other serious offenses and unless there is no other appropriate response;
(d) The well-being of the juvenile shall be the guiding factor in the consideration of her or his case. 17.2 Capital punishment shall not be imposed for any crime committed by juveniles.

17.3 Juveniles shall not be subject to corporal punishment.

17.4 The competent authority shall have the power to discontinue the proceedings at any time.

Commentary
The main difficulty in formulating guidelines for the adjudication of young persons stems from the fact that there are unresolved conflicts of a philosophical nature, such as the following:

(a) Rehabilitation versus just desert;
(b) Assistance versus repression and punishment;
(c) Reaction according to the singular merits of an individual case versus reaction according to the protection of society in general;
(d) General deterrence versus individual incapacitation.

The conflict between these approaches is more pronounced in juvenile cases than in adult cases. With the variety of causes and reactions characterizing juvenile cases, these alternatives become intricately interwoven.

It is not the function of the Standard Minimum Rules for the Administration of Juvenile Justice to prescribe which approach is to be followed but rather to identify one that is most closely in consonance with internationally accepted principles. Therefore the essential elements as laid down in rule 17.1 , in particular in subparagraphs (a) and (c), are mainly to be understood as practical guidelines that should ensure a common starting point; if heeded by the concerned authorities (see also rule 5), they could contribute considerably to ensuring that the fundamental rights of juvenile offenders are protected, especially the fundamental rights of personal development and education.

Rule 17.1 (b) implies that strictly punitive approaches are not appropriate. Whereas in adult cases, and possibly also in cases of severe offenses by juveniles, just desert and retributive sanctions might be considered to have some merit, in juvenile cases such considerations should always be outweighed by the interest of safeguarding the well-being and the future of the young person.

In line with resolution 8 of the Sixth United Nations Congress, rule 17.1 (b) encourages the use of alternatives to institutionalization to the maximum extent possible, bearing in mind the need to respond to the specific requirements of the young. Thus, full use should be made of the range of existing alternative sanctions and new alternative sanctions should be developed, bearing the public safety in mind. Probation should be granted to the greatest possible extent via suspended sentences, conditional sentences, board orders and other dispositions.

Rule 17.1 (c) corresponds to one of the guiding principles in resolution 4 of the Sixth Congress which aims at avoiding incarceration in the case of juveniles unless there is no other appropriate response that will protect the public safety.

The provision prohibiting capital punishment in rule 17.2 is in accordance with article 6, paragraph 5, of the International Covenant on Civil and Political Rights.

The provision against corporal punishment is in line with article 7 of the International Covenant on Civil and Political Rights and the Declaration on the Protection of All Persons from Being Subjected to Torture and Other Cruel, Inhuman or Degrading Treatment or Punishment, as well as the Convention against Torture and Other Cruel, Inhuman or Degrading Treatment or Punishment and the draft convention on the rights of the child.

The power to discontinue the proceedings at any time (rule 17.4) is a characteristic inherent in the handling of juvenile offenders as opposed to adults. At any time, circumstances may become known to the competent authority which would make a complete cessation of the intervention appear to be the best disposition of the case.

18. Various disposition measures
18.1 A large variety of disposition measures shall be made available to the competent authority, allowing for flexibility so as to avoid institutionalization to the greatest extent possible. Such measures, some of which may be combined, include:
(a) Care, guidance and supervision orders;
(b) Probation;
(c) Community service orders;
(d) Financial penalties, compensation and restitution;
(e) Intermediate treatment and other treatment orders;
(f) Orders to participate in group counseling and similar activities;
(g) Orders concerning foster care, living communities or other educational settings;
(h) Other relevant orders.

18.2 No juvenile shall be removed from parental supervision, whether partly or entire l y, unless the circumstances of her or his case make this necessary.

Commentary
Rule 18.1 attempts to enumerate some of the important reactions and sanctions that have been practiced and proved successful thus far, in different legal systems. On the whole they represent promising opinions that deserve replication and further development. The rule does not enumerate staffing requirements because of

possible shortages of adequate staff in some regions; in those regions measures requiring less staff may be tried or developed.

The examples given in rule 18.1 have in common, above all, a reliance on and an appeal to the community for the effective implementation of alternative dispositions. Community-based correction is a traditional measure that has taken on many aspects. On that basis, relevant authorities should be encouraged to offer community-based services.

Rule 18.2 points to the importance of the family which, according to article 10, paragraph 1, of the International Covenant on Economic, Social and Cultural Rights, is "the natural and fundamental group unit of society". Within the family, the parents have not only the right but also the responsibility to care for and supervise their children. Rule 18.2, therefore, requires that the separation of children from their parents is a measure of last resort. It may be resorted to only when the facts of the case clearly warrant this grave step (for example child abuse).

19. Least possible use of institutionalization
19.1 The placement of a juvenile in an institution shall always be a disposition of last resort and for the minimum necessary period.

Commentary
Progressive criminology advocates the use of non-institutional over institutional treatment. Little or no difference has been found in terms of the success of institutionalization as compared to non-institutionalization. The many adverse influences on an individual that seem unavoidable within any institutional setting evidently cannot be outbalanced by treatment efforts. This is especially the case for juveniles, who are vulnerable to negative influences. Moreover, the negative effects, not only of loss of liberty but also of separation from the usual social environment, are certainly more acute for juveniles than for adults because of their early stage of development.

Rule 19 aims at restricting institutionalization in two regards: in quantity ("last resort,,) and in time ("minimum necessary period"). Rule 19 reflects one of the basic guiding principles of resolution 4 of the Sixth United Nations Congress: a juvenile offender should not be incarcerated unless there is no other appropriate response. The rule, therefore, makes the appeal that if a juvenile must be institutionalized, the loss of liberty should be restricted to the least possible degree, with special institutional arrangements for confinement and bearing in mind the differences in kinds of offenders, offenses and institutions. In fact, priority should be given to "open" over "closed" institutions. Furthermore, any facility should be of a correctional or educational rather than of a prison type.

20. Avoidance of unnecessary delay
20.1 Each case shall from the outset be handled expeditiously, without any unnecessary delay.

Commentary
The speedy conduct of formal procedures in juvenile cases is a paramount concern. Otherwise whatever good may be achieved by the procedure and the disposition is at risk. As time passes, the juvenile will find it increasingly difficult, if not impossible, to relate the procedure and disposition to the offense, both intellectually and psychologically.

21. Records
21.1 Records of juvenile offenders shall be kept strictly confidential and closed to third parties. Access to such records shall be limited to persons directly concerned with the disposition of the case at hand or other duly authorized persons.

21.2 Records of juvenile offenders shall not be used in adult proceedings in subsequent cases involving the same offender.

Commentary
The rule attempts to achieve a balance between conflicting interests connected with records or files: those of the police, prosecution and other authorities in improving control versus the interests of the juvenile offender. (See also rule 8.) "Other duly authorized persons" would generally include among others, researchers.

22. Need for professionalism and training
22.1 Professional education, in-service training, refresher courses and other appropriate modes of instruction shall be utilized to establish and maintain the necessary professional competence of all personnel dealing with juvenile cases.

22.2 Juvenile justice personnel shall reflect the diversity of juveniles who come into contact with the juvenile justice system. Efforts shall be made to ensure the fair representation of women and minorities in juvenile justice agencies.

Commentary

The authorities competent for disposition may be persons with very different backgrounds (magistrates in the United Kingdom of Great Britain and Northern Ireland and in regions influenced by the common law system; legally trained judges in countries using Roman law and in regions influenced by them; and elsewhere elected or appointed laymen or jurists, members of community-based boards, etc.). For all these authorities, a minimum training in law, sociology, psychology, criminology and behavioral sciences would be required. This is considered as important as the organizational specialization and independence of the competent authority.

For social workers and probation officers, it might not be feasible to require professional specialization as a prerequisite for taking over any function dealing with juvenile offenders. Thus, professional on-the job instruction would be minimum qualifications.

Professional qualifications are an essential element in ensuring the impartial and effective administration of juvenile justice. Accordingly, it is necessary to improve the recruitment, advancement and professional training of personnel and to provide them with the necessary means to enable them to properly fulfil their functions.

All political, social, sexual, racial, religious, cultural or any other kind of discrimination in the selection, appointment and advancement of juvenile justice personnel should be avoided in order to achieve impartiality in the administration of juvenile justice. This was recommended by the Sixth Congress. Furthermore, the Sixth Congress called on Member States to ensure the fair and equal treatment of women as criminal justice personnel and recommended that special measures should be taken to recruit, train and facilitate the advancement of female personnel in juvenile justice administration.

PART FOUR

NON-INSTITUTIONAL TREATMENT

23. Effective implementation of disposition

23.1 Appropriate provisions shall be made for the implementation of orders of the competent authority, as referred to in rule 14.1 above, by that authority itself or by some other authority as circumstances may require

23.2 Such provisions shall include the power to modify the orders as the competent authority may deem necessary from time to time, provided that such modification shall be determined in accordance with the principles contained in these Rules.

Commentary
Disposition in juvenile cases, more so than in adult cases, tends to influence the offender's life for a long period of time. Thus, it is important that the competent authority or an independent body (parole board, probation office, youth welfare institutions or others) with qualifications equal to those of the competent authority that originally disposed of the case should monitor the implementation of the disposition. In some countries, a juge de l'execution des peines has been installed for this purpose.

The composition, powers and functions of the authority must be flexible; they are described in general terms in rule 23 in order to ensure wide acceptability.

24. Provision of needed assistance
24.1 Efforts shall be made to provide juveniles, at all stages of the proceedings, with necessary assistance such as lodging, education or vocational training, employment or any other assistance, helpful and practical, in order to facilitate the rehabilitative process.

Commentary
The promotion of the well-being of the juvenile is of paramount consideration. Thus, rule 24 emphasizes the importance of providing requisite facilities, services and other necessary assistance as may further the best interests of the juvenile throughout the rehabilitative process.

25. Mobilization of volunteers and other community services
25.1 Volunteers, voluntary organizations, local institutions and other community resources shall be called upon to contribute effectively to the rehabilitation of the juvenile in a community setting and, as far as possible, within the family unit.

Commentary
This rule reflects the need for a rehabilitative orientation of all work with juvenile offenders. Co-operation with the community is indispensable if the directives of the competent authority are to be carried out effectively. Volunteers and voluntary services, in particular, have proved to be valuable resources but are at present

underutilized. In some instances, the co-operation of ex-offenders (including ex-addicts) can be of considerable assistance.

Rule 25 emanates from the principles laid down in rules 1.1 to 1.6 and follows the relevant provisions of the International Covenant on Civil and Political Rights.

PART FIVE

INSTITUTIONAL TREATMENT

26. Objectives of institutional treatment
26.1 The objective of training and treatment of juveniles placed in institutions is to provide care, protection, education and vocational skills, with a view to assisting them to assume socially constructive and productive roles in society.

26.2 Juveniles in institutions shall receive care, protection and all necessary assistance-social, educational, vocational, psychological, medical and physical-that they may require because of their age, sex, and personality and in the interest of their wholesome development .

26.3 Juveniles in institutions shall be kept separate from adults and shall be detained in a separate institution or in a separate part of an institution also holding adults.

26.4 Young female offenders placed in an institution deserve special attention as to their personal needs and problems. They shall by no means receive less care, protection, assistance, treatment and training than young male offenders. Their fair treatment shall be ensured.

26.5 In the interest and well-being of the institutionalized juvenile, the parents or guardians shall have a right of access.

26.6 Inter-ministerial and inter-departmental co-operation shall be fostered for the purpose of providing adequate academic or, as appropriate, vocational training to institutionalized juveniles, with a view to ensuring that they do no leave the institution at an educational disadvantage.

Commentary
The objectives of institutional treatment as stipulated in rules

26.1 and 26.2 would be acceptable to any system and culture. However, they have not yet been attained everywhere, and much more has to be done in this respect.

Medical and psychological assistance, in particular, are extremely important for institutionalized drug addicts, violent and mentally ill young persons.

The avoidance of negative influences through adult offenders and the safeguarding of the well-being of juveniles in an institutional setting, as stipulated in rule 26.3, are in line with one of the basic guiding principles of the Rules, as set out by the Sixth Congress in its resolution 4. The rule does not prevent States from taking other measures against the negative influences of adult offenders, which are at least as effective as the measures mentioned in the rule. (See also rule 13.4)

Rule 26.4 addresses the fact that female offenders normally receive less attention than their male counterparts. as pointed out by the Sixth Congress. In particular, resolution 9 of the Sixth Congress calls for the fair treatment of female offenders at every stage of criminal justice processes and for special attention to their particular problems and needs while in custody. Moreover, this rule should also be considered in the light of the Caracas Declaration of the Sixth Congress, which, inter alia, calls for equal treatment in criminal justice administration, and against the background of the Declaration on the Elimination of Discrimination against Women and the Convention on the Elimination of All Forms of Discrimination against Women.

The right of access (rule 26.5) follows from the provisions of rules 7.1, 10.1, 15.2 and 18.2. Inter-ministerial and inter-departmental co-operation (rule 26.6) are of particular importance in the interest of generally enhancing the quality of institutional treatment and training.

27. Application of the Standard Minimum Rules for the Treatment of Prisoners adopted by the United Nations

27.1 The Standard Minimum Rules for the Treatment of Prisoners and related recommendations shall be applicable as far as relevant to the treatment of juvenile offenders in institutions, including those in detention pending adjudication.

27.2 Efforts shall be made to implement the relevant principles laid down in the Standard Minimum Rules for the Treatment of Prisoners to the largest possible extent so as to meet the varying needs of juveniles specific to their age, sex and personality.

Commentary
The Standard Minimum Rules for the Treatment of Prisoners were among the first instruments of this kind to be promulgated by the United Nations. It is generally agreed that they have had a world-wide impact. Although there are still countries where implementation is more an aspiration than a fact, those Standard Minimum Rules continue to be an important influence in the humane and equitable administration of correctional institutions.

Some essential protections covering juvenile offenders in institutions are contained in the Standard Minimum Rules for the Treatment of Prisoners (accommodation, architecture, bedding, clothing, complaints and requests, contact with the outside world, food, medical care, religious service, separation of ages, staffing, work, etc.) as are provisions concerning punishment and discipline, and restraint for dangerous offenders. It would not be appropriate to modify those Standard Minimum Rules according to the particular characteristics of institutions for juvenile offenders within the scope of the Standard Minimum Rules for the Administration of Juvenile Justice.

Rule 27 focuses on the necessary requirements for juveniles in institutions (rule 27.1) as well as on the varying needs specific to their age, sex and personality (rule 27.2). Thus, the objectives and content of the rule interrelate to the relevant provisions of the Standard Minimum Rules for the Treatment of Prisoners.

28. Frequent and early recourse to conditional release
28.1 Conditional release from an institution shall be used by the appropriate authority to the greatest possible extent, and shall be granted at the earliest possible time.

28.2 Juveniles released conditionally from an institution shall be assisted and supervised by an appropriate authority and shall receive full support by the community.

Commentary
The power to order conditional release may rest with the competent authority, as mentioned in rule 14.1 or with some other authority. In view of this, it is adequate to refer here to the "appropriate,' rather than to the "competent" authority.

Circumstances permitting, conditional release shall be preferred to serving a full sentence. Upon evidence of satisfactory progress towards rehabilitation, even offenders who had been deemed dangerous at the time of their institutionalization can be conditionally released whenever feasible. Like probation , such release may be conditional on the satisfactory fulfilment of the requirements specified by the relevant authorities for a period of time established in the decision, for example relating to "good behavior" of the offender, attendance in community programmes, residence in half-way houses, etc.

In the case of offenders conditionally released from an institution, assistance and supervision by a probation or other officer (particularly where probation has not yet been adopted) should be provided and community support should be encouraged.

29. Semi-institutional arrangements
29.1 Efforts shall be made to provide semi-institutional arrangements, such as half-way houses, educational homes, day-time training centers and other such appropriate arrangements that may assist juveniles in their proper reintegration into society.

Commentary
The importance of care following a period of institutionalization should not be underestimated. This rule emphasizes the necessity of forming a net of semi-institutional arrangements.

This rule also emphasizes the need for a diverse range of facilities and services designed to meet the different needs of young offenders re-entering the community and to provide guidance and structural support as an important step towards successful reintegration into society.

PART SIX

RESEARCH, PLANNING, POLICY FORMULATION AND EVALUATION

30. Research as a basis for planning, policy formulation and evaluation
30.1 Efforts shall be made to organize and promote necessary research as a basis for effective planning and policy formulation.

30.2 Efforts shall be made to review and appraise periodically the trends, problems and causes of juvenile delinquency and crime as well as the varying particular needs of juveniles in custody.

30.3 Efforts shall be made to establish a regular evaluative research mechanism built into the system of juvenile justice administration and to collect and analyze relevant data and information for appropriate assessment and future improvement and reform of the administration.

30.4 The delivery of services in juvenile justice administration shall be systematically planned and implemented as an integral part of national development efforts.

Commentary

The utilization of research as a basis for an informed juvenile justice policy is widely acknowledged as an important mechanism for keeping practices abreast of advances in knowledge and the continuing development and improvement of the juvenile justice system. The mutual feedback between research and policy is especially important in juvenile justice. With rapid and often drastic changes in the life-styles of the young and in the forms and dimensions of juvenile crime, the societal and justice responses to juvenile crime and delinquency quickly become outmoded and inadequate.

Rule 30 thus establishes standards for integrating research into the process of policy formulation and application in juvenile justice administration. The rule draws particular attention to the need for regular review and evaluation of existing programmes and measures and for planning within the broader context of overall development objectives.

A constant appraisal of the needs of juveniles, as well as the trends and problems of delinquency, is a prerequisite for improving the methods of formulating appropriate policies and establishing adequate interventions, at both formal and informal levels. In this context, research by independent persons and bodies should be facilitated by responsible agencies, and it may be valuable to obtain and to take into account the views of juveniles themselves, not only those who come into contact with the system.

The process of planning must particularly emphasize a more effective and equitable system for the delivery of necessary services. Towards that end, there should be a comprehensive and regular assessment of the wide-ranging, particular needs and problems of juveniles and an identification of clear-cut priori ties. In that connection, there should also be a co-ordination in the use of existing resources, including alternatives and community support that would be suitable in setting up specific procedures designed to implement and monitor established programmes.

APPENDIX D. United Nations Guidelines for the Prevention of Juvenile Delinquency

United Nations Guidelines for the Prevention of Juvenile Delinquency (The Riyadh Guidelines), G.A. Res. 45/112, annex, 45 U.N. GAOR Supp. (No. 49A), p. 201, U.N. Doc. A/45/49 (1990).

I. FUNDAMENTAL PRINCIPLES

1. The prevention of juvenile delinquency is an essential part of crime prevention in society. By engaging in lawful, socially useful activities and adopting a humanistic orientation towards society and outlook on life, young persons can develop non-criminogenic attitudes.

2. The successful prevention of juvenile delinquency requires efforts on the part of the entire society to ensure the harmonious development of adolescents, with respect for and promotion of their personality from early childhood.

3. For the purposes of the interpretation of the present Guidelines, a child-centered orientation should be pursued. Young persons should have an active role and partnership within society and should not be considered as mere objects of socialization or control.

4. In the implementation of the present Guidelines, in accordance with national legal systems, the well-being of young persons from their early childhood should be the focus of any preventive programme.

5. The need for and importance of progressive delinquency prevention policies and the systematic study and the elaboration of measures should be recognized. These should avoid criminalizing and penalizing a child for behavior that does not cause serious damage to the development of the child or harm to others. Such policies and measures should involve:
(a) The provision of opportunities, in particular educational opportunities, to meet the varying needs of young persons and to serve as a supportive framework for safeguarding the personal development of all young persons, particularly those who are demonstrably endangered or at social risk and are in need of special care and protection;
(b) Specialized philosophies and approaches for delinquency prevention, on the basis of laws, processes, institutions, facilities and a service delivery network aimed

at reducing the motivation, need and opportunity for, or conditions giving rise to, the commission of infractions;

(c) Official intervention to be pursued primarily in the overall interest of the young person and guided by fairness and equity;

(d) Safeguarding the well-being, development, rights and interests of all young persons;

(e) Consideration that youthful behavior or conduct that does not conform to overall social norms and values is often part of the maturation and growth process and tends to disappear spontaneously in most individuals with the transition to adulthood;

(f) Awareness that, in the predominant opinion of experts, labeling a young person as "deviant", "delinquent" or "pre-delinquent" often contributes to the development of a consistent pattern of undesirable behavior by young persons.

6. Community-based services and programmes should be developed for the prevention of juvenile delinquency, particularly where no agencies have yet been established. Formal agencies of social control should only be utilized as a means of last resort.

II. SCOPE OF THE GUIDELINES

7. The present Guidelines should be interpreted and implemented within the broad framework of the Universal Declaration of Human Rights, the International Covenant on Economic, Social and Cultural Rights, the International Covenant on Civil and Political Rights, the Declaration of the Rights of the Child and the Convention on the Rights of the Child, and in the context of the United Nations Standard Minimum Rules for the Administration of Juvenile Justice (The Beijing Rules), as well as other instruments and norms relating to the rights, interests and well-being of all children and young persons.

8. The present Guidelines should also be implemented in the context of the economic, social and cultural conditions prevailing in each Member State.

III. GENERAL PREVENTION

9. Comprehensive prevention plans should be instituted at every level of Government and include the following:

(a) In-depth analyses of the problem and inventories of programmes, services, facilities and resources available;

(b) Well-defined responsibilities for the qualified agencies, institutions and personnel involved in preventive efforts;

(c) Mechanisms for the appropriate co-ordination of prevention efforts between governmental and non-governmental agencies;

(d) Policies, programmes and strategies based on prognostic studies to be continuously monitored and carefully evaluated in the course of implementation;

(e) Methods for effectively reducing the opportunity to commit delinquent acts;

(f) Community involvement through a wide range of services and programmes;

(g) Close interdisciplinary co-operation between national, State, provincial and local governments, with the involvement of the private sector representative citizens of the community to be served, and labor, child-care, health education, social, law enforcement and judicial agencies in taking concerted action to prevent juvenile delinquency and youth crime;

(h) Youth participation in delinquency prevention policies and processes, including recourse to community resources, youth self-help, and victim compensation and assistance programmes;

(i) Specialized personnel at all levels.

IV. SOCIALIZATION PROCESSES

10. Emphasis should be placed on preventive policies facilitating the successful socialization and integration of all children and young persons, in particular through the family, the community, peer groups, schools, vocational training and the world of work, as well as through voluntary organizations. Due respect should be given to the proper personal development of children and young persons, and they should be accepted as full and equal partners in socialization and integration processes.

A. Family

11. Every society should place a high priority on the needs and well-being of the family and of all its members.

12. Since the family is the central unit responsible for the primary socialization of children, governmental and social efforts to preserve the integrity of the family, including the extended family, should be pursued. The society has a responsibility to assist the family in providing care and protection and in ensuring the physical and mental well-being of children. Adequate arrangements including day-care should be provided.

13. Governments should establish policies that are conducive to the bringing up of children in stable and settled family environments. Families in need of assistance in the resolution of conditions of instability or conflict should be provided with requisite services.

14. Where a stable and settled family environment is lacking and when community efforts to assist parents in this regard have failed and the extended family cannot fulfil this role, alternative placements, including foster care and adoption, should be considered. Such placements should replicate, to the extent possible, a stable and settled family environment, while, at the same time, establishing a sense of permanency for children, thus avoiding problems associated with "foster drift".

15. Special attention should be given to children of families affected by problems brought about by rapid and uneven economic, social and cultural change, in particular the children of indigenous, migrant and refugee families. As such changes may disrupt the social capacity of the family to secure the traditional rearing and nurturing of children, often as a result of role and culture conflict, innovative and socially constructive modalities for the socialization of children have to be designed.

16. Measures should be taken and programmes developed to provide families with the opportunity to learn about parental roles and obligations as regards child development and child care, promoting positive parent-child relationships, sensitizing parents to the problems of children and young persons and encouraging their involvement in family and community-based activities.

17. Governments should take measures to promote family cohesion and harmony and to discourage the separation of children from their parents, unless circumstances affecting the welfare and future of the child leave no viable alternative.

18. It is important to emphasize the socialization function of the family and extended family; it is also equally important to recognize the future role, responsibilities, participation and partnership of young persons in society.

19. In ensuring the right of the child to proper socialization, Governments and other agencies should rely on existing social and legal agencies, but, whenever traditional institutions and customs are no longer effective, they should also provide and allow for innovative measures.

B. Education

20. Governments are under an obligation to make public education accessible to all young persons.

21. Education systems should, in addition to their academic and vocational training activities, devote particular attention to the following:
(a) Teaching of basic values and developing respect for the child's own cultural identity and patterns, for the social values of the country in which the child is living, for civilizations different from the child's own and for human rights and fundamental freedoms;
(b) Promotion and development of the personality, talents and mental and physical abilities of young people to their fullest potential;
(c) Involvement of young persons as active and effective participants in, rather than mere objects of, the educational process;
(d) Undertaking activities that foster a sense of identity with and of belonging to the school and the community;
(e) Encouragement of young persons to understand and respect diverse views and opinions, as well as cultural and other differences;
(f) Provision of information and guidance regarding vocational training, employment opportunities and career development;
(g) Provision of positive emotional support to young persons and the avoidance of psychological maltreatment;
(h) Avoidance of harsh disciplinary measures, particularly corporal punishment.

22. Educational systems should seek to work together with parents, community organizations and agencies concerned with the activities of young persons.

23. Young persons and their families should be informed about the law and their rights and responsibilities under the law, as well as the universal value system, including United Nations instruments.

24. Educational systems should extend particular care and attention to young persons who are at social risk. Specialized prevention programmes and educational materials, curricula, approaches and tools should be developed and fully utilized.

25. Special attention should be given to comprehensive policies and strategies for the prevention of alcohol, drug and other substance abuse by young persons. Teachers and other professionals should be equipped and trained to prevent and

deal with these problems. Information on the use and abuse of drugs, including alcohol, should be made available to the student body.

26. Schools should serve as resource and referral centers for the provision of medical, counseling and other services to young persons, particularly those with special needs and suffering from abuse, neglect, victimization and exploitation.

27. Through a variety of educational programmes, teachers and other adults and the student body should be sensitized to the problems, needs and perceptions of young persons, particularly those belonging to underprivileged, disadvantaged, ethnic or other minority and low-income groups.

28. School systems should attempt to meet and promote the highest professional and educational standards with respect to curricula, teaching and learning methods and approaches, and the recruitment and training of qualified teachers. Regular monitoring and assessment of performance by the appropriate professional organizations and authorities should be ensured.

29. School systems should plan, develop and implement extracurricular activities of interest to young persons, in co-operation with community groups.

30. Special assistance should be given to children and young persons who find it difficult to comply with attendance codes, and to "drop-outs".

31. Schools should promote policies and rules that are fair and just; students should be represented in bodies formulating school policy, including policy on discipline, and decision-making.

C. Community

32. Community-based services and programmes which respond to the special needs, problems, interests and concerns of young persons and which offer appropriate counseling and guidance to young persons and their families should be developed, or strengthened where they exist.

33. Communities should provide, or strengthen where they exist, a wide range of community-based support measures for young persons, including community development centers, recreational facilities and services to respond to the special problems of children who are at social risk. In providing these helping measures, respect for individual rights should be ensured.

34. Special facilities should be set up to provide adequate shelter for young persons who are no longer able to live at home or who do not have homes to live in.

35. A range of services and helping measures should be provided to deal with the difficulties experienced by young persons in the transition to adulthood. Such services should include special programmes for young drug abusers which emphasize care, counseling, assistance and therapy-oriented interventions.

36. Voluntary organizations providing services for young persons should be given financial and other support by Governments and other institutions.

37. Youth organizations should be created or strengthened at the local level and given full participatory status in the management of community affairs. These organizations should encourage youth to organize collective and voluntary projects, particularly projects aimed at helping young persons in need of assistance.

38. Government agencies should take special responsibility and provide necessary services for homeless or street children; information about local facilities, accommodation, employment and other forms and sources of help should be made readily available to young persons.

39. A wide range of recreational facilities and services of particular interest to young persons should be established and made easily accessible to them.

D. Mass media
40. The mass media should be encouraged to ensure that young persons have access to information and material from a diversity of national and international sources.

41. The mass media should be encouraged to portray the positive contribution of young persons to society.

42. The mass media should be encouraged to disseminate information on the existence of services, facilities and opportunities for young persons in society.

43. The mass media generally, and the television and film media in particular, should be encouraged to minimize the level of pornography, drugs and violence portrayed and to display violence and exploitation disfavorably, as well as to avoid

demeaning and degrading presentations, especially of children, women and interpersonal relations, and to promote egalitarian principles and roles.

44. The mass media should be aware of its extensive social role and responsibility, as well as its influence, in communications relating to youthful drug and alcohol abuse. It should use its power for drug abuse prevention by relaying consistent messages through a balanced approach. Effective drug awareness campaigns at all levels should be promoted.

V. SOCIAL POLICY

45. Government agencies should give high priority to plans and programmes for young persons and should provide sufficient funds and other resources for the effective delivery of services, facilities and staff for adequate medical and mental health care, nutrition, housing and other relevant services, including drug and alcohol abuse prevention and treatment, ensuring that such resources reach and actually benefit young persons.

46. The institutionalization of young persons should be a measure of last resort and for the minimum necessary period, and the best interests of the young person should be of paramount importance. Criteria authorizing formal intervention of this type should be strictly defined and limited to the following situations:
 (a) where the child or young person has suffered harm that has been inflicted by the parents or guardians;
(b) where the child or young person has been sexually, physically or emotionally abused by the parents or guardians;
(c) where the child or young person has been neglected, abandoned or exploited by the parents or guardians;
(d) where the child or young person is threatened by physical or moral danger due to the behavior of the parents or guardians; and
(e) where a serious physical or psychological danger to the child or young person has manifested itself in his or her own behavior and neither the parents, the guardians, the juvenile himself or herself nor non-residential community services can meet the danger by means other than institutionalization.

47. Government agencies should provide young persons with the opportunity of continuing in full-time education, funded by the State where parents or guardians are unable to support the young persons, and of receiving work experience.

48. Programmes to prevent delinquency should be planned and developed on the basis of reliable, scientific research findings, and periodically monitored, evaluated and adjusted accordingly.

49. Scientific information should be disseminated to the professional community and to the public at large about the sort of behavior or situation which indicates or may result in physical and psychological victimization, harm and abuse, as well as exploitation, of young persons.

50. Generally, participation in plans and programmes should be voluntary. Young persons themselves should be involved in their formulation, development and implementation.

51. Government should begin or continue to explore, develop and implement policies, measures and strategies within and outside the criminal justice system to prevent domestic violence against and affecting young persons and to ensure fair treatment to these victims of domestic violence.

VI. LEGISLATION AND JUVENILE JUSTICE ADMINISTRATION

52. Governments should enact and enforce specific laws and procedures to promote and protect the rights and well-being of all young persons.

53. Legislation preventing the victimization, abuse, exploitation and the use for criminal activities of children and young persons should be enacted and enforced.

54. No child or young person should be subjected to harsh or degrading correction or punishment measures at home, in schools or in any other institutions.

55. Legislation and enforcement aimed at restricting and controlling accessibility of weapons of any sort to children and young persons should be pursued.

56. In order to prevent further stigmatization, victimization and criminalization of young persons, legislation should be enacted to ensure that any conduct not considered an offense or not penalized if committed by an adult is not considered an offense and not penalized if committed by a young person.

57. Consideration should be given to the establishment of an office of ombudsman or similar independent organ, which would ensure that the status, rights and

interests of young persons are upheld and that proper referral to available services is made. The ombudsman or other organ designated would also supervise the implementation of the Riyadh Guidelines, the Beijing Rules and the Rules for the Protection of Juveniles Deprived of their Liberty. The ombudsman or other organ would, at regular intervals, publish a report on the progress made and on the difficulties encountered in the implementation of the instrument. Child advocacy services should also be established.

58. Law enforcement and other relevant personnel, of both sexes, should be trained to respond to the special needs of young persons and should be familiar with and use, to the maximum extent possible, programmes and referral possibilities for the diversion of young persons from the justice system.

59. Legislation should be enacted and strictly enforced to protect children and young persons from drug abuse and drug traffickers.

VII. RESEARCH, POLICY DEVELOPMENT AND CO-ORDINATION

60. Efforts should be made and appropriate mechanisms established to promote, on both a multidisciplinary and an intradisciplinary basis, interaction and co-ordination between economic, social, education and health agencies and services, the justice system, youth, community and development agencies and other relevant institutions.

61. The exchange of information, experience and expertise gained through projects, programmes, practices and initiatives relating to youth crime, delinquency prevention and juvenile justice should be intensified at the national, regional and international levels.

62. Regional and international co-operation on matters of youth crime, delinquency prevention and juvenile justice involving practitioners, experts and decision makers should be further developed and strengthened.

63. Technical and scientific co-operation on practical and policy-related matters, particularly in training, pilot and demonstration projects, and on specific issues concerning the prevention of youth crime and juvenile delinquency should be strongly supported by all Governments, the United Nations system and other concerned organizations.

64. Collaboration should be encouraged in undertaking scientific research with respect to effective modalities for youth crime and juvenile delinquency prevention and the findings of such research should be widely disseminated and evaluated.

65. Appropriate United Nations bodies, institutes, agencies and offices should pursue close collaboration and co-ordination on various questions related to children juvenile justice and youth crime and juvenile delinquency prevention.

66. On the basis of the present Guidelines, the United Nations Secretariat, in co-operation with interested institutions, should play an active role in the conduct of research, scientific collaboration, the formulation of policy options and the review and monitoring of their implementation, and should serve as a source of reliable information on effective modalities for delinquency prevention.

APPENDIX E. Excerpts from The Jamaican Juveniles Act

The Juveniles Act[196]
[1st July, 1951]

1. This Act may be cited as the Juveniles Act.

Part I. *Preliminary*

2.—(1) In this Act—

"approved school" means a school approved by the Minister under section 35 or 36;

"approved school order" means an order made by a court sending a juvenile to an approved school;

"child" means a person under the age of fourteen years;

"children's home" means any institution, dwelling-house or other place where four or more children are boarded and maintained other than by a parent or lawful guardian, either gratuitously or for reward;

"children's officer" means a public officer designated by the Minister to be a children's officer for the purposes of this Act;

"contribution order" means an order made by a court under section 82 requiring any person to make contributions in respect of any juvenile committed to the care of a fit person or to an approved school;

"correctional officer" means an officer so designated by the Minister;

"the Council" means the Advisory Council established under this Act;

"fit person" includes the Minister, a local authority, children's home or any association of persons whether corporate or unincorporate;

"guardian", in relation to a juvenile, includes any person who, in the opinion of the court having cognizance of any case in relation to the juvenile or in which the juvenile is concerned, has for the time being the charge of or control over the juvenile;

"high security approved school" means the whole or such part of an approved school as may be declared to be a high security approved school by the Minister pursuant to section 77A;

"high security place of safety" means the whole or such part of a place of safety as may be declared to be a high security place of safety, by the Minister pursuant to section 77A;

---

[196]Transcript by Human Rights Watch.

"intoxicating liquor" means any fermented, distilled or spirituous liquor which cannot, save in certain specified circumstances, according to any enactment for the time being in force be legally sold without a licence;

"juvenile" means a person under the age of seventeen years;

"juvenile court" means any juvenile court established in accordance with the provisions of this Act;

"local authority" means the Parish Council of any parish or, in the cases of the parishes of Kingston and St. Andrew, the Kingston and St. Andrew Corporation;

"managers", in relation to an approved school established or taken over by a local authority or by a joint committee representing two or more local authorities, means the local authority or the joint committee, as the case may be, and in relation to any other approved school means the person for the time being having the management or control thereof;

"place of safety" means any place appointed by the Minister to be a place of safety for the purposes of this Act, or any hospital or other suitable place the occupier of which is willing temporarily to receive a juvenile;

"probation officer" means a person appointed under the Probation of Offenders Act, to be a probation officer;

"young person" means a person who has attained the age of fourteen years and is under the age of seventeen years.

(2) For the purposes of this Act any juvenile—

(a) who, having no parent or guardian, or having a parent or guardian unfit to exercise care and guardianship, or not exercising proper care and guardianship, is either falling into bad associations, or exposed to moral danger, or beyond control; or

(b) in respect of whom any offence mentioned in the First Schedule has been committed or attempted to be committed; or

(c) who is a member of the same household as a juvenile in respect of whom such an offence has been committed; or

(d) who is a member of the same household as a person who has been convicted of such an offense in respect of a juvenile,

shall be considered to be in need of care of protection; and the fact that a juvenile is found destitute, or is found wandering without any settled place of abode and without visible means of subsistence, or is found begging or receiving alms (whether or not there is any pretence of singing, playing, performing or offering anything for sale), or is found loitering for the purpose of so begging or receiving alms, shall, without prejudice to the generality or the provisions or paragraph (a), be evidence that he is exposed to moral danger.

3. It shall be conclusively presumed that no child under the age of twelve years can be guilty of any offence.

Part III. *Prevention of Cruelty to and Protection of Juveniles*

*   *   *   *

11.—(1) If it appears to a Justice on information on oath laid by any person who, in the opinion of the Justice is acting in the interests of a juvenile that there is reasonable cause to suspect—

(a) that the juvenile has been or is being assaulted, ill-treated or neglected in a manner likely to cause that juvenile unnecessary suffering; or

(b) that any offence mentioned in the First Schedule has been or is being committed in respect of the juvenile,

the Justice may issue a warrant authorizing any constable—

(I) to search for the juvenile and, if it is found that the juvenile has been or is being assaulted, ill-treated or neglected in any such manner, or that any such offence has been or is being committed in respect of him, to take him to and detain him in a place of safety; or

(ii) to remove the juvenile with or without search to a place of safety and to detain hm there,

until, in either such case, the juvenile can be brought before a juvenile court.

(2) A Justice issuing a warrant under this section may by the same warrant cause any person accused of any offence in respect of the juvenile to be apprehended and brought before a court of summary jurisdiction in order that proceedings may be taken against him according to law.

(3) Any constable authorized by warrant under this section to search for any juvenile, or to remove any juvenile with or without search, may enter (if need be by force) any house, building or other place specified in the warrant and may remove him therefrom.

(4) The constable executing any warrant issued under this section may be accompanied by the person laying the information, if that person so desires, and may also, if the Justice by whom the warrant is issued so directs, be accompanied by a duly qualified medical practitioner.

(5) It shall not be necessary in any information or warrant under this section to name the juvenile.

* * * *

13.—(1) Any constable or authorized person may bring before a juvenile court a juvenile in need of care or protection.

(2) For the purposes of this section the expression "authorized person" means—
(a) any probation officer or any children's officer;
(b) any person appointed by the Minister under section 7;
(c) any person appointed by the Minister on the recommendation of a welfare organization.

* * * *

14.—(1) A juvenile court before which any juvenile is brought under this Part, or before which is brought any juvenile in respect of whom any of the offences mentioned in the First Schedule has been committed, may, if satisfied that the welfare of the juvenile so requires, make an order—
(a) sending him to an approved school; or
(b) committing him to the care of any fit person, whether a relative or not, who is willing to undertake the care of him; or
(c) requiring his parent or guardian to enter into a recognizance to exercise proper care and guardianship; or
(d) placing him, either in addition to, or without making, any order under paragraph (b) or (c), for a specified period, not exceeding three years, under the supervision of a probation officer, or some other person to be selected for the purpose by the Minister.

(2) (a) If a juvenile court before which any juvenile is brought is not in a position to decide whether any or what order ought to be made under this section, it may make such interim order as it thinks fit for the juvenile's detention or continued detention in a place of safety, or for his committal to the care of a fit person, whether a relative or not, who is willing to undertake the care of him.

(b) Any interim order made under this subsection shall not remain in force for more than thirty days; but at any time within such period the court may, if it considers it expedient so to do, make a further interim order; so, however, that in no case shall any interim order or orders made under this subsection remain in force for more than sixty days after the date of the first order made under this subsection.

(c) If the juvenile court by which an interim order is made is satisfied on any occasion that, by reason of illness or accident, the juvenile is unable to appear personally before the court, any further interim order which the court has power to make on that occasion may be made in the absence of the juvenile.

*   *   *   *

Part IV. *Juvenile Courts and the Trial of Juvenile Offenders*

17. Arrangements shall be made by the Commissioner of Police for preventing a juvenile while detained in a police station, or while being conveyed to or from any criminal court, or while waiting before or after attendance in any criminal court, from associating with any adult, not being a relative, who is charged with any offence other than an offence with which the juvenile is jointly charged.

*   *   *   *

18.--(1) Where a person apparently a juvenile is apprehended, with or without warrant, and cannot be brought forthwith before a court, the officer or sub-officer of police in charge of the police station to which he is brought shall enquire into the case and may release him on a recognizance being entered into by him or his parent or guardian (with or without sureties) for such amount as will, in the opinion of the officer or sub-officer, secure his attendance upon the hearing of the charge, and shall so release him unless—

(a) the charge is one of homicide or other grave crime; or

(b) it is necessary in his interest to remove him from association with any reputed criminal or prostitute; or

(c) the officer or sub-officer has reason to believe that his release would defeat the ends of justice.

(2) Where a person apparently a juvenile is apprehended and is not released under subsection (1), the officer or sub-officer of police in charge shall cause him to be detained in a place of safety until he can be brought before a court.

*   *   *   *

19.—(1) Any court on remanding or committing for trial a juvenile who is not released on bail shall commit him to custody in a place of safety named in the commitment, to be there detained for the period for which he is remanded or until he is thence delivered in due course of law:

Provided that in the case of a young person it shall not be obligatory on the court so to commit him if the court certifies that he is of so unruly a character that he cannot safely be so committed, or that he is of so depraved a character that he is not a fit person to be so detained; and where the commitment so certifies he may be committed to such place, including a prison, as may be specified in the commitment warrant.

(2) A commitment under this section may be varied, or, in the case of a young person who proves to be of so unruly a character that he cannot safely be detained in such custody, or to be of so depraved a character that he is not a fit person to be so detained, revoked, by the court which made the order, or, if application cannot conveniently be made to that court, by any court having jurisdiction in the place where the court which made the order sat, and if it is revoked the young person may be committed to such place including a prison, as may be specified in the commitment warrant.

*   *   *   *

22.—(1) Courts, to be known as juvenile courts, shall be constituted in accordance with the provisions of the Second Schedule and, when so constituted and sitting for the purpose of exercising any jurisdiction conferred on them by this or any other enactment, shall be deemed to have, subject to the provisions of this Act, all the powers of a Resident Magistrate's Court, and the procedure in the juvenile court, subject to the provisions of the Act, shall be the same as in the Resident Magistrate's Court.

(2) The Governor-General may appoint, in respect of each juvenile court, a clerk and deputy clerk and such clerk and deputy clerk shall, in respect of the juvenile court to which they are so appointed, have all powers and perform all the duties which the clerk and deputy clerk have and perform in respect of a Resident Magistrate's Court:

Provided that it shall be lawful for any Clerk and Deputy Clerk, respectively, assigned under section 7 of the Judicature (Family Court) Act, to exercise the like powers and perform the like duties as aforesaid in respect of the juvenile court constituted by virtue of paragraph 4 of the Second Schedule.

(3) Without prejudice to the power to bring before a juvenile court by any other means any juvenile in need of care or protection, the attendance of a juvenile or of any other person before a juvenile court in accordance with the provisions of this Act may be enforced by the same officers, by the same process and in the same way as the attendance of persons before Justices may be enforced under the provisions of the Justices of the Peace Jurisdiction Act.

(4) Juvenile courts shall sit as often as may be necessary for the purpose of exercising any jurisdiction conferred on them by or under this or any other enactment.

(5) (a) A juvenile court shall sit in such place or places as may from time to time be specified under paragraph 3 of the Second Schedule as the place or places in which such court shall sit.

(b) Where no place is specified under paragraph 3 of the Second Schedule as the place in which a juvenile court shall sit, the juvenile court shall sit either in a different building or room from that in which sittings of courts other than juvenile courts are held, or on different days or at different times from those on which sittings of such other courts are held.

(6) No person shall be present at any sitting of a juvenile court except—

(a) members and officers of the court, and any authorized person as defined in section 13;

(b) parties to the case before the court, their counsel, solicitors, and witnesses giving or having given their evidence, and other persons directly concerned with the case;

(c) *bona fide* representatives of newspapers or news agencies;

(d) such other persons as the court may specially authorize to be present.

(7) Where a juvenile is brought before a juvenile court is shall be the duty of such court to explain to him in as simple language as possible the reason for his being before the court.

(8) Where a juvenile is charged before a juvenile court with any offence it shall be the duty of the court to ascertain the defence, if any, of the juvenile so

as to put, or assist the juvenile and his parents or guardian in putting, such questions to any witness as appear to be necessary.

(9) Where a juvenile is charged with any offence and admits the offence, or the court is satisfied that the offence has been proved, the court shall record a finding to that effect and before sentencing the juvenile shall obtain such information as to his general conduct, home surrounding, school record, and medical history as may enable it to deal with the case in the best interests of the juvenile. For the purpose of obtaining such information or for special observation the court may from time to time remand the juvenile on bail or in custody.

(10) An appeal shall lie from any decision of a juvenile court in the same manner and subject to the same procedure as an appeal from a Resident Magistrates Court.

*   *   *   *

24.—(1) A juvenile court sitting for the purpose of hearing a charge against, or an application relating to, a person who is believed to be a juvenile may, if it thinks fit so to do, proceed with the hearing and determination of the charge or application notwithstanding that it is discovered that the person in question is not a juvenile.

(2) Where a juvenile court has remanded a juvenile for information to be obtained with respect to him or for special observation, any juvenile court sitting in the same parish or place—

    (a) may in his absence extend the period for which he is remanded, so however, that he appears before a court at least once in every thirty days;

    (b) when the required information has been obtained, may, subject to any right of appeal provided by this Act, deal with him finally,

and where the court by which he was originally remanded has recorded a finding that he is guilty of an offence charged against him, it shall not be necessary for any court which subsequently deal with him under this section to hear evidence as to the commission of that offence, except in so far as may be considered that such evidence will assist the court in determining the manner in which he should be dealt with.

*   *   *   *

29.—(1) Sentence of death shall not be pronounced on or recorded against a person convicted of an offence if it appears to the Court that at the time when the offence was committed he was under the age of eighteen years, but in place thereof the court shall sentence his to be detained during Her Majesty's pleasure, and, if so sentenced, he shall, notwithstanding anything in the other provisions of this Act, be liable to be detained in such place (including, save in the case of a child, a prison) and under such conditions as the Minister may direct, and while so detained shall be deemed to be in legal custody.

(2) A juvenile shall not be sentenced to imprisonment, whether with or without hard labour, for any offence, or be committed to prison in default of payment of any fine, damages or cost.

(3) Where a young person is convicted of an offence specified in the Third Schedule and the court is of opinion that none of the other methods in which the case may legally be dealt with is suitable, the court may sentence the offender to be detained for such period as may be specified in the sentence. Where such a sentence has been passed the young person shall, during that period notwithstanding anything in the other provisions of this Act, be liable to be detained in such place (including a prison) and on such conditions as the Minister may direct and while so detained shall be deemed to be in legal custody.

(4) The Governor-General may release on licence any person detained under subsection (1) or (3). Such licence shall be in such form and contain such conditions as the Governor-General may direct, and may at any time be revoked or varied by the Governor-General. Where such licence is revoked the person to whom it relates shall return forthwith to such place as the Governor-General may direct, and if he fails to do so may be arrested by any constable without warrant and taken to such place.